Reporting on Crime

Bringing Great Police Work to the Courtroom

Second Edition

Aaron Pinson, MA

John Day, MA

Reporting on Crime
Second Edition
Aaron Pinson, MA
John Day, MA

ISBN: 979-8-90333-867-2

Arizona Book Publishing LLC
www.ArizonaBookPublishing.com

Table of Contents

Dedications

This book is dedicated to a number of people who have inspired me for part or all of my life:

- My father, who taught me one of life's greatest lessons: Never quit… keep moving forward…
- Dave Pikka, who consistently showed me what 'right' looked like: Ethically, morally, and professionally. His example always encouraged me to do more, to do and be better, to do it the right way.
- Captain Roy Day, who was willing to spend years mentoring a very naïve young officer.
- Our families, who have endured countless sleepless nights… missed family events… and the stress of living with the law enforcement profession.
- Rachel Day, for her unlimited support, and the many years of being a single parent while I was deployed.
- My field trainers, Lt. Doug James and SGT. Kenneth Moberly, who spent their time instilling habits that will last a lifetime.
- My co-author, who without his support and involvement, this book would be nothing more than just a passing thought.
- Velena Phillips, a survivor of a violent crime, who reminds us of what we should all strive to be…
- Finally, to those of you who spend their days, nights, weekends, and holidays keeping the rest of us safe… God Bless.

Letter From Velena Phillips

Velena Phillips, Survivor of Violent Crime

October 2, 2005. This was a Sunday and a day that is forever etched in my memory and my son's. On this day my son, Ethan Ingram, and I faced one of the most terrifying moments of our lives, as we were stranded on the side of the highway and a man tried to force us into his vehicle. He forced my son to witness despicable acts. No matter how hard I fought this man, he threw my little Ethan into speeding traffic three times, yet Ethan never gave up. With every ounce of his small body, Ethan fought fiercely to protect me, returning to the battle again and again, even as cars raced by. He watched my clothes being torn open, exposing me and subjecting me to unimaginable violations.

Despite the horror unfolding before him, on that day Ethan, at just five, earned the title of Superman from me as he showed a strength beyond his years and fought to survive the terror no child should ever witness. But even with his bravery, no one stopped to help us, no one wanted to get involved, and I couldn't get my phone open to work. Ethan fought so bravely for me and alongside me that the evil disguised as a man, eventually did panic and ran, but I was still able to get his license plate number. I called 911 and relayed it to them. Ethan and I were exhausted laying on the road struggling to get back inside our car.

When we were at the brink, and no one helped us, it was Aaron Pinson who arrived not only as a law enforcement office but also as a guardian of hope and compassion. His unwavering kindness in one of our darkest hours exemplified the very best of what it means to wear the badge. He covered me, protecting my dignity when I was in shock, and most importantly he made sure my son, who had witnessed the worst, felt safe. He made sure my son, who fought bravely, felt safe and heard, and just how proud of Ethan he was. He spoke to him with such gentleness, helping him through the process of giving a statement and helped him through the hours of everything that needed to be done, and never left his side until the situation was secure and the man had been caught and was being brought back to Aaron at the office to be interviewed and dealt with. Not only did he bring justice to the man who attacked us, but he brought us peace in a moment of terror. And he did all of this when I could barely comprehend the magnitude of what happened. The compassion and professionalism Aaron showed that day are forever etched into our lives. You see that day my son was named Superman by me, but so too, was Aaron Pinson.

Aaron is a reminder that every officer… no matter the challenges they face… has the power to change lives in profound ways. There will be days when the uniform feels heavy, when the world seems to overlook the sacrifices made. You will face days that test every fiber of your being and you'll wonder if the burden is worth it, but to those who serve, please know there will always be someone who desperately needs you, a woman under attack… or a child forced to endure the unimaginable, fighting just to survive.

Your presence, your bravery, your dedication can change the course of someone's life, just as Aaron's changed ours. Your courage in the face of darkness, your resolve to keep going when it seems impossible, will forever be the reason that hope survives.

To Aaron Pinson, who embodies the true spirit of service, and to every officer who gives their all, know that you are seen, you are appreciated, and you make a difference that will never be forgotten.

And to all of the LEO's and first responders there that night, you too were noticed and very much appreciated. Ethan and I thank you so much for your service that night and every night.

-Velena Phillips, 2005, Phelps County, MO

Forward

There are countless reasons why writing a quality police report matters...but it's rarely treated like a priority. Most training officers don't gravitate toward report writing because it's not the "sexy" part of the job; that's just the reality. Policy and procedure, warrant service, vehicle pursuits, firearms training...those are the high-adrenaline topics that get attention. Writing, by contrast, feels tedious. But here's the truth: it's one of the most critical skills an officer can develop.

This book isn't a textbook... it's a practical guide for officers who are new to the profession or struggling with documentation. It was intended to be a supplement to an officer's statute book; put them together and a new recruit should be able to write a great report... because when citizens suffer loss, injury, or trauma, they depend on the officer's ability to write clearly and accurately. That report becomes the foundation for accountability. Take car accidents, for example: insurance companies don't care about drama, they care about facts. They rely on the officer's report to determine fault, while it's the officer's role to identify probable contributing circumstances.

If the report is vague, sloppy, or incomplete, it can derail the entire process. Teaching someone to write well isn't glamorous. It's not a day at the range or a high-speed chase. While it may be the least trained skill in the department, it's often the most important.

A well-written report can shield an officer from lawsuits, internal discipline, and criminal charges. A poorly written one can do the opposite. In cases like Graham v. Connor (1989), courts emphasized that use-of-force decisions must be evaluated based on what the officer knew at the time... not what others assume in hindsight. But if the officer fails to document what they knew, what they saw, and what they did, that legal protection evaporates. In short, a report isn't just paperwork… it's the officer's testimony… the officer's voice when they're no longer in the room. And depending on how it's written, it can be the difference between being defended by counsel… or being charged by a prosecutor.

Today's political climate has changed everything; being able to write and justify the decisions made has never been more important. Unfortunately, that has not changed the job, and there are people in communities you work… who will need your services. Writing has never been more important than it is today… where political influences may try and manipulate what officers do, say, or how they perform; so, understanding how to "justify" what's done is absolutely critical.

Every year new responsibilities get added on to the officer's job requirements; making this climb seem almost unsurmountable. There will always be those who plot against individual officers. However, understanding how to logically stack demonstrative factors together… leading to the decisions at a scene… will keep officers safe; regardless of the personal or political influences of the day. It is our goal to teach officers these skills; equipping them with the armor and sword, so they can withstand the attacks of modern policing. The evolving landscape of law enforcement demands not only courage and physical prowess but also the ability to articulate decisions with precision.

The police report is like an officer's shield… protecting them from political and professional criticism.

In today's charged climate, where every action is scrutinized, the written word becomes a shield… an armor of accountability. Officers must wield it skillfully, explaining their actions, justifying their choices, and ensuring transparency.

Whether it's a use-of-force report, an incident summary, or a court testimony, a properly written narrative matters. It's often the bridge between action and understanding, and it can sway public opinion, legal outcomes, and even an officer's own mental well-being. Political influences can ripple through law enforcement. Sometimes they're like gusts of wind, pushing against the sails of justice. Other times, they're like tidal waves, threatening to capsize the ship.

Officers must remain steadfast, anchored by principles and guided by policy. Justifying their actions isn't about bending to political whims; it's about standing firm in the face of adversity. Job requirements pile up like layers of sediment, each year adding weight to the officer's load. It's like climbing a mountain with no summit…yet they persist. But here's the secret: Each added responsibility is a foothold. Each report, each interaction, contributes to their expertise. And as they ascend, they gain a broader perspective, a clearer view of the landscape they protect.

There are those who plot against officers… whether it's through misinformation, or political maneuvering, or violence. It's a harsh reality… but the ability to stack demonstrative factors logically is the sword. It's the skill of weaving evidence, context, and intent into a cohesive narrative… and it's the difference between vulnerability and resilience. As educators, mentors, and advocates, we empower officers. We sharpen their quills and teach them to wield their pens with purpose. The armor we provide isn't just Kevlar…it's the ability to withstand scrutiny, to stand tall even when the storm rages. It's knowing that their words matter, that they echo through time and shape the legacy of policing. Now, it's your turn, our time has come and gone, and we are passing the baton. All officers get is one chance to write a report, and unfortunately there will always be… just one more person… who depends on you. So… don't embarrass us… and don't f#@k this up.

About the Authors

Aaron Pinson

Mr. Pinson holds an Associate's degree of Science in Criminal Justice Administration and a Bachelor's degree of Arts in Criminal Justice Administration. He also carries a Master of Arts degree in Business and Organizational Security Management. He is a combat veteran, having served with the 24th Infantry Division during Desert Shield/Storm, as an Army Sapper.

Mr. Pinson is also a former police officer and served for both municipalities and a county sheriff's department. He has held various positions ranging from that of Patrolman, Field Training Officer, Traffic Crash Reconstructionist, and Patrol Supervisor.

Mr. Pinson has taught Criminal Justice and Homeland Security classes for Excelsior College, and he has taught for the United States Army's Military Police School; teaching the Basic and Advanced Antiterrorism Courses.

John Day

Mr. Day holds a Bachelor of Arts in History with a minor in Russian Language from the University of Missouri-Rolla. Mr. Day also holds a Masters in National Security with an Emphasis in Terrorism.

He is a combat veteran of multiple deployments to Iraq and Afghanistan.

Mr. Day is also a former police officer and has served for both local and a county sheriff's department. He has held various positions ranging from: Patrolman, Field Training Officer, Traffic Crash Reconstructionist, Patrol Supervisor, SWAT team member, SWAT Sniper, K-9 Officer, and Detective.

He has also served in Military Law Enforcement as a Watch Commander, Patrolman, and Military Investigator. Mr. Day has instructed at United States Army Military Police School teaching at the Joint Non-Lethal Weapons Instructor's Course.

Mr. Day is currently on active duty and is assigned to a special operation unit.

The author(s) encourage and solicit comments regarding the book; to include suggestions for the next edition. The author(s) can also make themselves available for assistance in this area.

PART ONE: Police Report Writing

A Case For Quality

This is my Way of Arguing for Well Written Reports

The art of police report writing is like a dance between fact, context, and the weight of responsibility. It's like seasoned blues musicians rifting on their guitars; it's a symphony of syntax and bullet points.

New recruits often hear the refrain: "Read other reports, practice, and give it time." And there's truth in that advice. It's like learning to play slide guitar... awkward at first, but eventually, your fingers find the right frets.

But here's the twist: The school of hard knocks isn't a gentle tutor. She's more like a grizzled sergeant who barks, "Write it again, rookie!" And so, officers learn...their words etched with sweat, adrenaline, and the echoes of sirens. Picture this... a courtroom, the air thick with tension and a skilled defense attorney steps forward, wielding words like a rapier. They dissect the officer's report, exposing gaps, contradictions, and missed beats. It's a humbling experience... one that leaves an indelible mark.

The officer's ass, metaphorically speaking, is handed to them; but from that bruised ego blooms growth. They vow to sharpen their quill, to craft narratives that withstand legal scrutiny.

Mistakes are the ink blots of progress. Officers who stumble... whose reports crumble under cross-examination... become the cautionary tales. Their missteps ripple through the precinct like whispered warnings; and so, others learn. They dissect those flawed reports, extracting lessons. They study syntax, clarity, and the art of weaving facts into airtight narratives. It's like reverse engineering a Joe Banamassa blues riff… breaking it down to its soulful core.

Every officer should aim higher, not just because of legal battles or the specter of internal affairs. It's about honoring the badge, the oath, and the community. So, they write. They revise. They seek feedback. And in the quiet hours, when the station hums with fluorescent light, they polish their prose, because excellence isn't a destination… it's a relentless pursuit.

Imagine a world where police reports read like poetry… clear, concise, and compelling; where each word carries weight, each sentence stands tall. That's the goal. To wield the pen like a conductor's baton, leading the orchestra of justice. And when the final note is struck, it echoes through courtrooms, boardrooms, and history itself.

Police narratives are the novels of law enforcement; picture this… A dimly lit room, and a single desk lamp casting shadow. An officer hunches over their keyboard, weaving words into existence. Their report isn't just ink on paper; it's a narrative… a chronicle of events that unfolded under streetlights and sirens. Like a novelist, they set the scene: "On a chilly night, in the heart of the city…" They introduce characters… the stoic officer, the agitated suspect, the witness with secrets. And they build tension… the adrenaline surge, the split-second decisions…the stakes rising like crescendoing blues chords.

Exposition: These are the detective's clues… expository elements sneak in… the who, what, when, where, and why. It's like laying out evidence on a detective's corkboard. "The suspect, identified as one Mr. John Doe, was seen fleeing…," or, "At approximately 02:37 hours, officers responded to a disturbance call…" These details anchor the report, grounding it in reality. They're the signposts along the narrative highway.

Persuasion: This is the prosecutor's pitch; here's where it gets interesting. A police report isn't just a sterile recitation of facts; it's a subtle nudge toward justice. The officer chooses words carefully, "The suspect's erratic behavior posed an imminent threat."

They lay the groundwork for the prosecutor's courtroom performance. It's like tuning a guitar...each string resonating with intent.

Technical Precision: This in the crash reconstruction sonata. The reconstruction of a motor vehicle crash... oh, it's a symphony of math, physics, and skid marks. Tire coefficients, impact angles, momentum vectors... they all dance in the margins of the report. It's not just writing; it's translating chaos into equations. The officer becomes a crash scene maestro.

The Hybrid Style: Think of this as the jazz improv in blue ink; police reports defy categorization. They're jazz... a fusion of styles, improvisation within structure. The may officer channel Hemingway's terse sentences, stripped of excess. Or maybe they channel Faulkner, with winding prose, and unraveling mysteries. Sometimes, they might even channel Dr. Seuss: "One perp, two perp, red perp, blue perp."

The Unseen Heroes: These are the editors and proofreaders; behind the scenes, there's an unsung chorus...the editors. They wield red pens like conductors' batons. "Officer, your syntax is off-key. Harmonize those paragraphs!" And the report transforms... a polished gem, ready for courtrooms and archives.

The Credibility Quotient: Credibility isn't just a buzzword... it's the currency of law enforcement. Officers trade in it daily, like poker chips at a high-stakes table. When an officer explains an incident... whether to a fellow officer, a suspect, or a courtroom audience... their credibility is on the line. It's like tuning a guitar before a blues jam; every string matters. So, they choose their words carefully, marshal facts, weave context, and build a narrative that stands up to scrutiny.

Safety and Survival: Officers must stay safe. It's not just a mantra; it's a lifeline. Going home at the end of the day isn't negotiable. But safety isn't a solo act. It's a duet with situational awareness, tactical training, and split-second decisions; and sometimes, it's knowing when to holster the pen and draw the weapon.

The Burden of Policing: Investigating crimes, arresting suspects, justifying actions... it's a juggling act. Imagine spinning plates on a tightrope. And then there's the courtroom… a battleground where words clash like swords. Prosecutors rely on those reports… the ink-stained scrolls…to build their case. The officer becomes a storyteller, a bard recounting the saga of law and disorder.

Explaining the Unexplainable: It's the challenge of explaining chaos. Picture an overturned car, shattered glass, and witnesses in shock. The officer steps into this fractured reality. Their report becomes a bridge… a lifeline for future selves. Years later, in a courtroom, they'll stand there recalling the scene. The report, their lifeline, will refresh their memory. Preliminary hearings, depositions… the legal ballet begins, and the officer, like a blues guitarist riffing on memory chords, plays their part.

Civil Trials and Criminal Odes: Trials… both criminal and civil are like grand symphonies: The witnesses testify; attorneys spar; and the judge conducts. The officer's report? It's the sheet music… the notes that harmonize with truth, and when the jury leans in, they'll hear the melody of justice. Police reports are like the ink-stained chronicles of law enforcement…their pages filled with the raw material of justice.

The Scribe's Duty: Recording Reality… Imagine an officer at the scene… a flurry of activity, voices overlapping, adrenaline humming. Amid this chaos, they become the scribe, capturing details like a photographer framing a shot. From the mundane (license plate numbers) to the profound (a victim's tearful account), it all finds its place in the report. And that old adage… "If it's not in the report, it didn't happen" … hangs over them like a neon sign.

The Memory's Lifeline: Refreshing recollections years later, in a courtroom, the officer stands… a sentinel of truth. The report becomes their lifeline, a bridge to the past. "Officer, what happened on that fateful night?" They flip open the report, and suddenly, the scene reassembles… the scents, the sounds, the urgency. Its memory resurrected.

Justification and Clarity: The report isn't just ink on paper, it's a shield. It justifies an officer's words, actions, and silence. "Why did you approach the suspect?" The report whispers the answer: "His erratic behavior posed an imminent threat." It's the difference between clarity and confusion, between a blues riff and a cacophony.

The Lieutenant's Office: This is where shadows lurk…a place of stern glances and raised eyebrows. It's where officers tread carefully, like tightrope walkers. "Officer, care to explain this discrepancy?" And there it is…the report, dissected under fluorescent lights. The officer sweats, hoping their words hold up.

Reasonable Justification: This is an officer's North Star…reasonable justification…those two words guide officers. It's the compass in the fog; the lighthouse on rocky shores. It keeps them on the straight and narrow, away from murky waters; it becomes part of the rhythm…the blues of policing.

The Report's Weight And Impact: Police reports aren't mere ink on paper… they're the threads that weave through the fabric of justice. Each word carries weight, each sentence echoes in courtrooms and legal chambers. Punitive fines? They're like thunderclaps… a reckoning for actions deemed malicious or negligent. When an officer's report lacks precision, it's akin to handing the opposing side a loaded weapon.

The New Recruit's Dilemma: Picture a fresh-faced officer, just out of the academy. They hold their pen like a sword, ready to document the world. But here's the twist; they lack the foundational knowledge. Field training programs, often a whirlwind of practical experience, may not emphasize the art of writing. New recruits read reports, mimicking top-notch officers, but it's like learning to play blues guitar by listening to Eric Clapton… it helps, but it's not enough.

Professional writers in blue; law enforcement officers are indeed professional writers. Their words ripple through time, shaping investigations, court proceedings, and public perception, and those outside professionals? They're like literary critics, dissecting every phrase. A sloppy report isn't just a typo; it's a chink in the armor.

The defense attorney's lens… masters of scrutiny… read reports with a magnifying glass. Their perception matters. If they see sloppiness, they pounce. Imagine the courtroom: "Officer, your report lacks clarity. Your credibility wavers." Suddenly, the officer's ammunition… those words on paper… misfires.

Precision and Preparedness: Submitting a sloppy report is like handing a suspect a loaded gun. It's a misstep…and an avoidable one. Submitting a sloppy police report is tantamount to sharing ammunition with a suspect during a gun battle; it just should not be done because the officer will see those rounds again.

The art of writing… especially in law enforcement…I s a multifaceted skill that extends far beyond mere ink on paper.

The Silent Judgment of Words: People do indeed judge based on writing. It's like sizing up a blues guitarist by the way they handle their fretboard. If the notes are off-key, the perception shifts. Spelling, grammar, and clarity… they're the chords of credibility. When an officer's report wavers, so does their reputation.

The Unseen Origins of Literacy: Spelling methods…memorization or phonics…shape our linguistic DNA. Some words take root; others wither. But here's the twist; an officer's ability to write isn't just about spelling…it's about wielding language with precision. It's the difference between a blues scale and a discordant note.

The Symphony of Reports: Imagine a symphony hall filled with readers… supervisors, prosecutors, defense attorneys, judges… the audience of justice. Each report is a movement… an opus of facts, context, and narrative. And when the final note fades, impressions linger. "Officer Bluesman's report lacked coherence," whispers the prosecutor. "Their credibility wavers."

The Art of Filling Holes: A well-written report isn't just a summary; it's a blueprint. It fills gaps, bridges inconsistencies. "Why wasn't the this done?" The report answers: "Due to exigent circumstances, officer safety took precedence." Suddenly, the scene becomes clearer…the shadows illuminated.

Pride in the Quill: Officers, take pride in your quill. Each stroke matters. Whether it's a traffic stop or a homicide investigation, your words echo. So, focus on the report. It's your legacy…the blues riff you leave behind.

The Blueprint For Novices: because starting points matter. For new officers grappling with report writing, an outline is like sheet music…a guide to composing their symphony of facts. It's not about perfection; it's about building a foundation. The first blues lick on a guitar might falter, but it's a start.

The why behind the madness… understanding the "why" is like tuning an instrument. It's not enough to know where to place your fingers… you must grasp the harmony. Law enforcement professionals do this, because words are the chords of justice. They resonate in courtrooms, boardrooms, and archives. When an officer writes, they're not just documenting; they're shaping reality. Each report is a ripple… a stone dropped into the pond of truth.

Reproducibility: this is the encore Performance, imagine a blues guitarist nailing a riff during a live show. The crowd roars. But can they replicate it tomorrow? Next week? Officers, too, need consistency. The method isn't a one-hit wonder; it's the backbone of their career. "Officer, can you explain your actions on that night?" The report becomes their encore…a familiar melody, played flawlessly.

The symphony of clarity… spelling and grammar… those grace notes… are essential. They're the difference between a haunting ballad and a cacophony. And yes, people judge. A sloppy report isn't just ink; it's a reflection… an impression etched in memory.

"Officer, your credibility wavers."

Suddenly, the blues riff stumbles. So… focus on the report.

Tucson Police, Shooting at Lowes

On November 29th, 2021, Tucson Police Officer Ryan Remington shot and killed an elderly man in a wheelchair who was accused of shoplifting and aggravated robbery. The incident sparked widespread outrage due to the victim's age and condition. Consequently, the police chief, the city mayor, and the media all condemned the officer's actions; before an investigation even started. It's often said that if something isn't documented in a report, it didn't happen. Therefore, police officers should be diligent in their reporting, as it serves as their shield and armor against the scrutiny of woke leadership and the liberal media, who profit from the suffering of others.

Before the investigation even began, the police chief condemned the officer's actions. This created two significant issues: It potentially tainted the jury pool and subtly influenced the investigators. The police chief's comments put all investigators on notice, as they knew how he felt and they had to work with him afterward. The police chief holds significant power over their careers, including lateral transfers and promotions, which could be affected by their findings. While this may not be a problem if the findings are clear-cut, if the decisions are on a razor's edge, they will likely align with the chief's initial remarks.

Chief's Actions

Citizens rely on the education, training, and experience of their police chief; therefore, the reflections of a police chief on an officer's actions carry significant weight with the citizenry… specifically to potential jury members, who will be chosen from that group of people.

According to the reporting, Chief Magnus spoke publicly the day after the shooting and made the following statements:

✓ "I am deeply troubled by Officer Remington's actions."

✓ "His use of deadly force in this incident is a clear violation of department policy and directly contradicts multiple aspects of our use of force training."

Chief Magnus potentially interfered with potential jurors… who rely on him as citizens… to present accurate information; yet he made these statements before the investigation had a chance tp report definitive results.

Mayors Response

The citizens of Tucson elected Mayor Romero to lead them, and… just like with the police chief… they rely on her for accurate, responsible information. Most people don't have law-enforcement training; their understanding of police work often comes from television and movies. Because of that, they (not everybody) naturally trust what their leaders say. When an elected official publicly condemns an officer before the investigation is complete, it shapes public perception in a way that can be deeply damaging.

The prosecutor released a video explaining the decision not to pursue a fourth grand jury. It's important to remember that each prior grand jury gave the State another opportunity to refine and strengthen its case. In that same video, the prosecutor acknowledged that her office lacked personnel with the education, training, and experience to handle a case of this complexity. As a result, they brought in outside counsel… attorneys from Los Angeles… to take over the prosecution.

A major part of this story comes down to cost. Three separate grand juries were convened… each one requiring time, resources, and preparation. Leadership's public comments created the real possibility of a change of venue, which would have driven expenses even higher. The prosecutor's office then hired outside counsel from Los Angeles because they admitted they lacked the internal expertise to handle a case of this complexity. And on top of all that, any potential lawsuit filed by Remington for wrongful termination or defamation would add yet another layer of financial exposure. In legal terms, this is exactly how a case "snowballs." The check kept getting bigger and bigger.

Courts have long recognized how leadership missteps can inflate costs. In Sheppard v. Maxwell (1966), the U.S. Supreme Court held that prejudicial public statements by officials can compromise a fair trial and force courts to take expensive corrective measures… like venue changes or retrials. Similarly, in Gentile v. State Bar of Nevada (1991), the Court acknowledged that prosecutors and public officials have a heightened duty to avoid comments that could taint proceedings, precisely because those comments can trigger costly legal consequences.

The pattern is the same here: once leadership speaks prematurely, the system pays for it… financially, legally, and publicly.

Mayor Romero publicly described Officer Remington's actions as:

- "Unconscionable and indefensible"
- "Untenable" (as referenced by Remington's attorney criticizing her early comments)
- She also stated that:
- She gave her full support to the Pima County Attorney's Office as it proceeded with its investigation.

These statements were made less than 24 hours after the shooting, before the investigation had been completed, which Remington's attorney later called "outrageous" and "inflammatory".

These statements, made by Executive leadership cost the residents of Tucson thousands of dollars; potentially millions.

Prosecutor's actions

Prosecutors claimed they lacked the education, training, or experience to prosecute a police officer, so they contracted with others... from Los Angeles to prosecute the case.

Because the prosecutors did not have confidence in their own office staff... they contracted with outsiders... which in itself costs the citizens of Tucson thousands of dollars. Moreover, they put Remington through 3 Grand Juries... one of which... they intentionally mislead the 1st Grand Jury. If Remington chooses to sue the city they will potentially cost the citizens of Tucson thousands more.

Three Grand Juries were held, and their findings are listed below:

Grand jury #1...August 2022

Finding: Indictment issued

- The first grand jury indicted Remington for manslaughter in August 2022.
- However, this indictment was later thrown out by a judge because prosecutors had presented misleading or incomplete information to the grand jury.

Grand Jury #2...January 2023

Finding: No Bill (No Indictment)

- A second grand jury reviewed the case and refused to indict, issuing a "no bill"

Grand Jury #3...January 2025

Finding: No Bill (No Indictment)

- According to Ingram (2025) A third grand jury again declined to indict Remington, issuing another "no bill" and ending the Pima County Attorney's attempts to prosecute the case.

- Pima County Attorney Laura Conover stated her office would not seek further review after the third rejection.

Some might argue that Remington's report did not work, or play its part, because his career ended, city leadership condemned his action, and he went through three grand juries. I would argue that the report served its purpose. Let's consider some of the mitigating factors that may have come under scrutiny.

Tucson's leadership… Police Chief Chris Magnus and Mayor Regina Romero… handled the situation poorly. On the very day of the shooting, with the investigation barely underway, both publicly declared Officer Remington's actions "unforgivable."

Making such definitive statements before the facts were established placed the city in a legally vulnerable position. If Remington were later cleared or a grand jury declined to indict, those premature comments could expose the city to significant liability. In effect, their remarks ended Remington's four-year law enforcement career (no evidence available or found to suggest otherwise) on the spot… yet a grand jury ultimately chose not to indict him.

The Report's Mitigating Factors

- What was he doing when he got the call; where was he at; date; and time
- What were the initial reports of offender's violations
- Offender had a knife and had committed an aggravated robbery… or a violation of some similar crime… involving the theft of merchandise while using a knife to threaten staff/customers

- Offender had left Walmart and was on an electric scooter, heading to Lowes
- Officer contacts offender; identifies himself
- Asks him to stop; tells him to stop; orders him to stop
- Orders offender to drop the knife
- Offender refuses to follow instructions and ignores orders
- Document any statements like, "The only way to stop me is to shoot me" (or any comments of a similar nature)
- Remington knows the offender has a knife and was willing to use it
- Reminton does not know if the offender is armed with a firearm, but there is no doubt the offender is willing to threaten or use violence… because it already happened with the knife
- Remington does not know if the offender can get out of the scooter, but people are seen using scooters or wheelchairs for which they can get up and walk; so just because he is in a scooter… does not mean he is stuck there
- Remington knows that time is a factor because with every second… they get closer to the entrance to Lowes
- Remington knows he has a responsibility to the safety of other citizens… and they are getting closer
- K-9 was not an option, because no dog was at the scene and they would be inside Lowes before a K-9 would get there
- Taser was not a reasonable option, because he is in a scooter, which would interfere with the spread of the probes…making it an ineffective option
- No law requires officers to intentionally put their own lives in danger; so wrestling with the offender is not an option

- At the moment the offender entered the lobby… a terrible chose had to be made… but it's a decision forced by the offenders' actions and unwillingness to follow commands
- Suicide by cop… is a real thing
- Remington had to know, if the offender was allowed to enter another store, and threatens or hurts another citizen, then he is responsible and accountable for what happens because he failed to act

People may be upset with the outcome of that call for service (wasn't really a call for service, because he was working secondary employment at the time) but there were no "good" answers; when the offender forces law enforcement to protect the lives of others.

A full assessment of the incident must account for the mitigating factors confronting Officer Remington at the time. When he received the information, he was working secondary employment and responding in real time to reports that the offender had just committed an aggravated robbery…stealing merchandise while brandishing a knife and threatening staff and customers. The offender had already fled Walmart on an electric scooter and was heading toward Lowe's, a second occupied business.

Upon contact, Remington identified himself, issued repeated commands to stop, and ordered the offender to drop the knife. Those commands were ignored. The offender reportedly made statements consistent with "suicide by cop," a phenomenon recognized in both policing literature and case law as a legitimate operational concern. Remington knew the offender was armed with a knife and had already demonstrated a willingness to use or threaten violence.

He could not know whether the offender also possessed a firearm, nor could he assume the scooter prevented mobility; officers routinely encounter individuals who stand, flee, or fight despite appearing disabled. Time was a critical factor, as every second brought the offender closer to the entrance of Lowe's and the citizens inside.

Remington had a legal duty to protect those citizens, and no reasonable alternatives were available: no K-9 was on scene, a Taser was unlikely to be effective due to the scooter's structure interfering with probe spread, and no law requires an officer to endanger himself by attempting to physically wrestle an armed suspect. As the offender crossed into the lobby, Remington faced a rapidly evolving, life-threatening situation in which the suspect's refusal to comply forced a terrible decision.

Under Graham v. Connor (1989), the Supreme Court held that use-of-force must be judged from the perspective of a reasonable officer on the scene, not with "the 20/20 vision of hindsight," and that officers are not required to choose the least intrusive option...only a reasonable one. Likewise, Tennessee v. Garner (1985) recognizes that deadly force may be justified when an officer has probable cause to believe a suspect poses a significant threat of death or serious physical harm to the officer or others.

Arizona law mirrors this standard, permitting deadly force when an officer reasonably believes it is necessary to protect against an immediate threat. In this case, allowing an armed, noncompliant offender... already willing to threaten violence... to enter another crowded store would have exposed innocent people to grave danger. Remington understood that failing to act could make him legally and morally accountable for whatever happened next.

People may be upset with the outcome, but the truth is that there were no "good" options that day. The offender's actions, refusals, and escalating danger left only hard choices, and the law requires those choices to be judged through the standard of reasonableness... not the comfort of hindsight. Some may claim Remington's report was flawed simply because leadership reacted poorly, but the fact remains: he is not in prison. That alone shows the report accomplished what it was supposed to do.

A police report is not just a narrative about what happened to someone else; it is also the officer's legal shield. It documents what the officer saw, what they knew, what they did, and what they could not safely do. In Remington's case, the report fulfilled its purpose by preserving the facts as he understood them in the moment.

Ferguson Vs. St. Louis Metropolitan Police Department

During the height of the Ferguson riots in August 2014, a separate officer-involved shooting occurred only a few miles from the epicenter of the unrest. Although often conflated with events in Ferguson, this incident fell under the jurisdiction of the St. Louis Metropolitan Police Department (SLMPD), not Ferguson PD.

This incident offers a far better example of how leadership… both law enforcement and elected officials…should communicate in the aftermath of a critical event. Executive leaders owe the public transparency and reassurance, but they must also rely on their own education, training, and experience to speak responsibly. That means addressing the situation without compromising anyone's rights or prejudging the outcome of an investigation.

On August 19, 2014, SLMPD officers responded to reports of a man threatening people with a knife. Upon arrival, officers encountered 23-year-old Kajieme Powell, who had reportedly stolen items from a nearby convenience store and was behaving erratically. Witnesses and video evidence indicated that Powell advanced toward officers while shouting, "Shoot me now. Kill me now." As he closed distance with the knife in hand, officers opened fire.

At the scene, Chief Sam Dotson addressed the public and the media. His message emphasized three key points:

- The immediate threat to the community had been neutralized.
- A formal investigation into the shooting was already underway.
- Despite the tragedy, officers have the right to return home safely at the end of their shift.

This incident unfolded just 3–4 miles from Ferguson, adding to the already volatile atmosphere in the region.

While the circumstances differed significantly from the Michael Brown shooting, the proximity in time and location caused the two events to be discussed side-by-side in national conversations about policing, mental health crises, and use of force.

The SLMPD shooting stood in clear contrast to the Ferguson incident in terms of how leadership communicated with the public. Farrington (2014) of MPR News and Levy (2014) of US News reported, Chief Sam Dotson emphasized that an investigation was underway, reassured the community that the immediate threat had been resolved, and encouraged people to continue with their daily lives. At no point did he criticize or prejudge the officers' actions while the facts were still being gathered. His remarks avoided influencing public perception of the case, did not contaminate the potential jury pool, and placed no pressure on investigators to reach a particular conclusion.

While investigators were at the scene, the municipality's police chief addressed the community through the media. He reassured them that the threat was over, mentioned that an investigation was underway, and emphasized that, despite the tragedy, all his officers had the right to return home safely at the end of their shift. The offender was black, but unlike the Ferguson riots, the unrest did not spread to this community, likely due to the chief's timely and transparent communication. In contrast, during the Ferguson shooting, there was no leadership statement and "no written report" generated by the involved officer.

Progression From Recruit to Seasoned Officer

Seasoning a new patrol officer isn't an exact science, but there is a well-understood progression in the profession. Here's the clearest way to frame it, based on common training standards and what veteran cops know from experience; based on what I have observed.

1. Field Training (FTO Phase): 3–6 months

- This is where the recruit learns policies, radio traffic, report writing, officer safety, and basic street sense.
- They're still thinking step-by-step, not fluidly.

2. First Year on Their Own: Learning the Job

- They can function independently, but they're still green.
- Decision-making is slower.
- They rely heavily on training rather than instinct.
- They're still learning how to read people, neighborhoods, and patterns.

3. True "Seasoning": 3–5 years

- Develop real situational awareness
- Learn to de-escalate effectively
- Understand body language and pre-attack indicators
- Know the difference between lawful, necessary, and smart
- Can handle chaotic scenes without freezing or overreacting
- Build confidence without becoming reckless

By this stage, they've seen enough calls…domestics, mental health crises, fights, traffic stops, foot pursuits, and the occasional truly dangerous moment…to understand the rhythm of the street.

4. Fully Mature Officer 7–10 years:

- Calm under pressure
- Efficient with paperwork and investigations
- Trusted by supervisors
- A mentor to younger officers
- Able to see danger before it happens

This is also the point where they've usually experienced at least one major incident that permanently shapes their judgment.

Bottom Line

- Competent: 1 year
- Seasoned: 3–5 years
- Fully mature street cop: 7–10 years

Seasoning a police officer isn't just a matter of time; it's exposure, mentorship, leadership, and surviving the moments that permanently reshape how you see the job. Officer Remington had roughly four years on the street, and he had to make his decision based on the training, experience, and judgment he had at that point in his career. He did not have the benefit of four decades of accumulated wisdom to draw from, and it is unreasonable to expect a four-year officer to think or react like a forty-year veteran.

Knowing this, Chief Magnus brought more than four decades of experience to the job. Yet there seemed to be an unspoken expectation that Officer Remington, who had only four years on the street should have made the same decisions a forty-year veteran would have made. That is not how law enforcement works.

Officers act based on their education, training, and accumulated experience, applying those factors to rapidly evolving situations, state statutes, and case law. Expecting a relatively new officer to think and respond like someone with forty years in the profession is unrealistic, unfair, and ultimately dangerous.

Starting a Report

This first section in a police report should accomplish a number of goals and is arguably one of the most important. First it should tell the reader the date and time that the officer first learned of the incident or responded to the scene. In some cases, this sets a timeline that can be used later, such as in a drug interdiction case where the length of the detention may be a factor.

In 2005, a delayed sexual assault report was received by the Phelps County Sheriff's Department, Rolla, MO. The incident occurred in July of 1988. This timeline also tells the Prosecutor whether or not they need to blow the dust off of old law books to see which laws were in effect at the time of crime; or if the Statute of Limitations (determined later) for that crime has come and gone. Second, the first section describes where the officer is going, or the location of the offense. This is important because it sets up the jurisdiction for the court; and some cities rest between different counties (Sullivan, MO is split between Crawford and Franklin Counties). Finally, the first section can help explain the officer's actions when they initially arrived at the scene; this can be considered a justification clause.

The crucial information that a dispatcher gives officers, while they are responding to a scene, should be explained in the first section; again, it's all about justification. The details may vary from information about a suspect, to facts about the area, to information about past calls, or to issues about the residence/area. This will validate the reason an officer exited their squad car with their weapon drawn, or going to the trunk and getting out the barrier tape.

In review, the first section establishes the time frame, jurisdiction, and the reason law enforcement is called in the first place. When combined, these factors establish the foundation for prosecution of the offender, without this information the case is headed south for the winter.

Throughout this document a domestic violence report will be generated, which will be in italics, as an example of a police report. At the end, the complete text of the report will be published. While some of the actions discussed would not normally be taken during this type of investigation, it's done to demonstrate various ideas, techniques and examples. Again, there is a distinct gap between academy time and field training; and this is an attempt to bridge that gap.

There are a number of perspectives used in the creation of a police report; however, experience suggests a 1st person be used while drafting a police report. For that reason, a 1st person approach is used for the demonstration. Moreover, at the time of this report… film cameras were in full swing… while digital cameras were just becoming available. Today, body worn cameras are common place, and for departments that are accredited... they are required. In either case, the importance of these tools is critical, and it will be discussed in detail… later.

Call For Service

On December 17, 2005, at approximately 12:30 PM, Detective Day and I were "summoned" to 12345 South Highway 63 Rolla, MO in reference to a domestic disturbance. Dispatch explained that a female had called them and reported that her husband had hit her, adding that the caller was now locked in the bathroom. While on the way to the scene we were informed, by radio, that the caller claimed that her husband had a knife, and had been chasing her with it before she locked the door to the bathroom. Dispatch went on to explain, that there was a violent history at this residence, adding that the husband has been arrested three times, each time for domestic assault. Dispatch continued and stated that the caller had not hung up the phone, and that they could still hear a lot of yelling in the background.

The stage is now in set. Officer(s) have just "justified" certain actions that may or may not happen, but the tone of the call has been set. This has in essence set the reader up for what was to happen next. Everything in this section of the report should be considered, even the word choice.

Words are interesting, and even synonyms don't carry the same weight, some bring a different flavor to the report. In this case, we choose the word "summoned" over "dispatched", even though they are both true, because summoned suggest that the officers involved were "asked" to respond. Both are good choices and either would be true statements, but summoned is the best choice; it helps set the mood.

One caution applies to word choice, and it applies throughout the report. If the author is not sure of the meaning of the word...choose another word. Don't overwrite the report. Don't use words just to sound important, because that's not what this is all about. Remember the scene in "Blazing Saddles" when a main character says, "golly gee, you sure do use your tongue purdier than a two-dollar whore."

Who Did You Contact... First

The second section is about the first person that you contact when you arrive at the scene; the reporting party, witness, etc... Keep in mind that this person may be identified on the phone, or at some other location, and may also be a witness, the victim, or the suspect. It's important to remember that the way in which you identify people in a report is just as important as the process itself.

A report should be fluid, and it should also be easily understood. Nobody should have to flip back several pages to find the portion of the report that fully identifies the person you are dealing with.

If nothing else this is a courtesy that the writer provides to the reader. Our suggestion would be to identify everyone by name, date of birth, social security number, address, contact telephone number, and e-mail address, using a bullet type format.

John W. Doe
DOB: 01-01-79
SSN: 123-45-6789
(573) 123-4567

It's recognized that not all of this information can be obtained, but if it can then include it. If an officer cannot obtain this information, then report what's available. This way the reader has all of the information to identify a person in one area. This will reduce confusion and help the reader, especially when you are dealing with several people with the same last name. Your case may be assigned to another officer, sent to another department, or to the detective bureau and being able to identify a person quickly can greatly aid in the investigation and the prosecution. Another aspect of this section of the report is the condition of the reporting party or the victim, whomever they happen to be. What they said, how they said it, and what their condition happens to be is important.

Example: an officer responds to the scene of a domestic, where the aggressor has fled. During the interview the officer should take note of their condition, and their actions: Were there any injuries, were they crying, what are the conditions of their surroundings. Statements of what happened are nice, but it's even better to make observations that corroborate their statements.

Keep in mind that people have more than one sense: people hear, people smell, people see. Your report should be complete; it should spell out everything that was noticed. The observations made by the reporting officer can be used to solve crimes quickly; after they have been reported. Many officers like to read the reports of other officers to learn what has occurred during the prior shifts. Observations that are quickly and accurately detailed in a report benefit the investigation.

Officers who read the reports might be able to assist you either from prior knowledge or from future acts; remember knowledge is power.

As a side note, new recruits should remember to use "paragraphs" throughout the report. This helps the reader track a narrative as they continue through the report. It's suggested that new recruits change paragraphs whenever they change person, topic, location, etc.… This may sound ridiculous to some, but police reports have been published as one complete paragraph… or using just capital letters. There have been reports published, which documented the arrest of a violent felon, and the entire report was one paragraph, which only contained six or seven brief statements. Those days are long gone; today's police reports come with sworn statement notifications, and statements about the use of body worn cameras…which will be detailed later.

Example: *Upon arrival at the scene, just moments in front of Detective Day, I observed a white male standing in the front yard of the residence wearing nothing but "heart" covered boxers. As I got out, I noticed that the male had what appeared to be red scratches all over his chest, he was breathing heavy, and his face was red and blotchy; he appeared very angry. I could clearly see that the man had nothing in his hands, and after he turned around, he walked towards me.*

The male was identified as:

John W. Doe
DOB: 01-01-79
SSN: 123-45-6789
(573) 123-4567

Mr. Doe stated that he was tired of that "bitch" and added that he was going to divorce "her sorry ass." When asked, Mr. Doe stated that he had found a letter in his wife's coat pocket and added that for the last few weeks she has been having an affair. Mr. Doe explained that after he read the letter, he "just lost it", grabbing her off the couch by her hair. Mr. Doe went on, stating that he couldn't seem to stop himself, adding that he hit her three or four times in the face, which is when she kneed him in the "balls." Mr. Doe continued, stating that she ran into the bathroom and locked the door.

At this point both officers should have a general idea of what had taken place, as one-sided as it is, but there is more to do. Once Mr. Doe had made his first statement, officers had to ask him some **clarifying** questions. In this case there isn't a lot to ask, but in others this may be the key to the entire investigation: Who's lying, who's not, and who's going to be spending the night in jail.

During drug interdiction stops, involving commercial tractor trailers, it's the clarifying questions that will lead to consent to search, arrest, and the seizers of large quantities of drugs, guns, or human trafficking. Clarifying questions is one of the single most important steps that the investigating officer can use; in the report, it reads something like this.

When asked, Mr. Doe stated that his wife never raised a hand to him, adding that he never really gave her a chance. Mr. Doe explained that the scratches on his chest were done when she was trying to wiggle out of his grasp, adding that the only reason he let go was because "the bitch kneed me in the balls."

When asked, Mr. Doe admitted that he had picked up a kitchen knife but had quickly decided that she was not worth it. Mr. Doe claimed that he had stuck the knife in the living-room wall before walking outside.

At this point Mr. Doe was detained in double-locked handcuffs, and placed into the rear of my patrol car, pending the outcome of the investigation.

Statements... Who Said What

Statements are great, and officers should write down or know what the people are saying; the accusations they are raising. Moreover, statements help the officers and prosecutors connect the dots; proving their cases beyond a reasonable doubt. Quotes are great…no other way to put it. Sometimes the remarks that are made by people just can't be ignored; paraphrasing just doesn't do them justice. Example, after a man has just been arrested for beating his girlfriend, he makes a spontaneous utterance announcing, "Man, that bitch will never forget me now" or "I stole the car and ran her over." Officers will find themselves quietly yelling yahoo…keep on talking buddy.

Keep in mind that if an officer uses a quote that is extremely long, and they didn't write it in their notes, their credibility may be questioned later. Juries are human, and if an officer appears to have a superhuman memory the jurors may not believe the officer's testimony. Officers should remember the Miranda equation:

Custody + Interrogation = Miranda

When suspects make those types of statements your report should have a line or two explaining that you advised them of their Miranda rights (remember, if it's not in the report it did not happen).

Written statements have another use, which is to buy officer's time. When officers first arrive on a scene it may be chaotic, with people running about and inadvertently damaging the crime scene. If officers hand out statements, with pens to write with, they have now given them something to do; keeping them in one spot. Officers can even ask them to wait there until you contact them again; getting their statement(s). This keeps the statement writer occupied in one spot and allows officers time to organize; it also controls a scene, keeps those who are at the scene from fighting, or potentially hiding evidence.

Statements are important, and if everyone is still at the scene when officers arrive, the report will flow rather well. The problem is that this is not always the case, so statements should be written in your narrative after the officer has talked to, or confronted, the person. In short, keep the report in order.

As to statements, officers should be searching for the answers to six specific questions: Who, what, when, where, why, and how. Each person may not know the answers to all of those questions, but they should be addressing the questions/answers that they do know. They should each be explaining: Who they are; who did they see committing the crime; who is the victim of the crime; what did they see; where did it happen (specific locations); when did it happen; how did it happen; and if possible, why did it happen. Each of these questions is equally important, and at some point, will have to be answered.

However, the answer to "why" could potentially lead to "criminal intent." Intent is not an element for all crimes, but it is for the vast majority; where it's not included as an element of a crime, its often replaced with criminal negligence. Criminal negligence would be written in statutes like "involuntary manslaughter," which is where the suspect did something so stupid, any "reasonable" person could anticipate the results. Example: In Missouri there was a juvenile who wanted to play a prank on his buddy, who was riding on a bicycle with "mag" wheels. The juvenile threw a stick in the front wheel, and the victim ended up cart-wheeling over the bike; landing on his face. The juvenile involved had "zero" intent to hurt his best friend, but the outcome was obvious. So, why often equals intent, and intent leads to conviction(s).

So, what type of statements does the officer take? That depends on the situation, and the officer needs to make that call. Verbal statements are good, written statements are better, and video confessions are better yet; combinations of these are the best.

Moreover, today's policing often involves body worn cameras. Give the suspect as many opportunities to confess as you can, or as many opportunities to lie.

In one instance during an interrogation, a suspect started to pray out loud, begging God for forgiveness. The Officer allowed him to finish praying. Later, the officer questioned him again about what happened. Before the interrogation was complete, the suspect repeated the incident in front of a digital recorder. During the trial, the officer admitted that the suspect had confessed three times; all of the statements were admitted into court and the suspect was convicted. Take that same case today… changing it up a bit… an officer could get a verbal statement, a written statement, and the recording on the body worn camera; however, officers should ensure the written report is supported by the body worn camera. Don't be the officer that gets jammed up because the report doesn't reflect what's recorded on the body worn camera.

Stories change. Sometimes it's not a bad idea to video tape (digitally record) their statements. It is quite possible to find the victim of domestic violence changing their story, and/or the statement that he or she gave right after being beaten. Don't be surprised when this occurs; a written or digitally recorded statement becomes even more important. This happens when the victim tells himself/herself that the incident was their fault and realizes that they are still in love with their better half. Officers should not be caught off guard when the victim goes to the police chief, lodging a formal complaint, and reporting that the officer lied or twisted what they said. Frankly, new officers should anticipate this happening, because it probably will, but the body-worn camera can protect everyone involved.

Example: Late one night an officer was dispatch to a local hospital because a report of domestic violence. While at the hospital, the officer interviewed the victim and took digital images of her injuries. The victim made a verbal statement, a written statement, and when asked, repeated the incident in front of a small digital video camera (pre-body worn camera days). Before leaving the officer asked her if she understood why he had asked her for the video. She didn't understand the need, so the officer explained. The officer told her that before she decided to complain that he had twisted what had been said, or before she decided to lie on the stand, the officer wanted her to remember the video. She nodded in understanding.

The victim's best friend had brought her to the hospital and followed the officer out. As the officer turned around, she gave him a big hug. The officer was a little shocked, and it must have been apparent. The friend explained that the victim had recanted statements in the past, and added that the video would ensure that she followed through with the charges. The "Paul Harvey" version includes the victim's upcoming marriage to the assailant, and his 2nd degree assault plea agreement that the suspect made with the prosecutor. In that case, everyone turned out happy: The victim, the suspect, and the prosecutor. When the officer heard what happened, he found myself smiling…so even the officer was happy.

Statements, written, videotaped, or body worn cameras, can save officers from needless troubles; supporting their written justification. It can ensure that the person who committed the crime has the opportunity to go to jail. A video-taped statement will ensure that the prosecutors have enough evidence to go to trial, and the ability to challenge the new version of their statements.

A final thought to consider when handing out written statement forms, is that the person completing the statement needs something to write with. Sometimes these people may have blood or other contaminants on their hands and let's not forget those people who like to chew on pens while they think about what they are writing.

Obviously, officers do not want to give them their favorite pen, which they received as a present upon graduation from the academy. First, officers probably will not get their pen back. Second, if they do, they will have to sanitize the pen before they can use it again. Pens can be obtained from a variety of sources; businesses will sometimes have pens in cups designed as an advertisement for any customer to take, or officers can purchase a box of pens for under a couple of dollars. Any way you slice it, don't give up your sidearm or your pen; both of which, under the right conditions, can cost you your career.

In this case, the officer already had Mr. Doe's statement, but they still needed to speak with Mrs. Doe, who's the victim, and get her side of the story. In addition, officers need to note any injuries that she may have and get her medical treatment if she needs it. Keep in mind that in some cases an officer may have contacted her while he was speaking to Mr. Doe. This is a technical issue that a department policy or the situation will dictate. In order to keep things simple, both officers interviewed Mr. & Mrs. Doe together.

As a side note, some new officers may not be able to sympathize with the victim; coming off as stoic… or robotic.

One piece of advice… which is effective… but may come of cold or sneaky. However, the moment officers learn to "fake sincerity" their connections will go smoother… this could potentially work against supervisors too… just saying.

After Officer's Arrival

In most cases finding the victim will not be all that hard, and in all honesty, they may find you. Normally, dispatch has already told you where the victim is, and finding him or her is easy. Once the officer is with the victim, or as soon as the scene is secure, dispatch needs to be made aware of that; in some cases, an ambulance may have been staged nearby waiting for an opportunity to treat the injured. As soon as the "all clear" sign is given, they will roll in to give you a hand.

In addition, there may be others in the area who need to be identified: The victim, children, and other witness. In each case the identification is the same as described above; there is no reason to reinvent the wheel. The exception may be juveniles, and departmental policy will dictate the process (normally just identified with initials). Including the juvenile's information in the narrative of the report is not on its face a problem. The problem with this is if the record clerk happens to give the report to a citizen, and that information is not blocked out… (i.e., redacted)… "that's all bad." In addition, the standardization of officer reports will only increase the appearance of professionalism. Over time it will also allow officers to write their reports faster because the more you write reports the easier they become.

The next portion of the report reads something like this:

Once Mr. Doe was secured in the back of my patrol car, we attempted to locate the victim. The front door to the residence was open, and after I announced our arrival, we waited a few moments before entering their home. When nobody answered or came to the door we entered the residence, noting that the entire living-room was in disarray. The pillows for the couch were on the floor, an end-table was lying on its side, pictures had been knocked off the wall, and there was a large knife stuck in the wall near the front door.

Point of interest: Don't use general terms like disarray without explanations of what was in disarray...give examples. Moreover, the knife in the door supports the statement that the suspect already gave us. We are one step closer to locking the door on his cell. This same idea applies if officers are in an uncomfortable position and choose to search something for "officer-safety reasons." In those cases, and they happen, simply explain the details which make it dangerous; don't just write that something was done for officer safety reasons and not explain the justification. Officers include specific details in a report so when they are questioned later, they remember the details, and the questions may come years later. Officers will never stop justifying their actions; the courts are intended to ferret out answers, when citizens accuse them of violating their rights. It's illegal for a citizen to resist an arrest... even if they feel it's an illegal arrest; the courts are designed for citizens to bring their grievances. So, officers should expect and prepare for this eventuality, because it's probably going to happen.

The report continues...

There was a hallway that ran to the left of the living-room, and we continued to yell as we made our way down the hall. A short time later a female opened the door at the end of the hall and stated that her husband had hit her. The female's right eye was almost completely closed, the results of bruising and swelling. The bruise ranged in color from dark purple to pink. In addition, her nose looked out of place, as if it was swelling on one side. Furthermore, I noticed that her top lip was bruised and swollen; with the same color scheme described above (ensure to take pictures of the victim's injuries; and if the case is serious enough repeat pictures a week later. (They may be needed to show bruise progression).

Pic 1… the female

The female was identified as:

Jane M. Doe
DOB: 12-12-78
SSN: 321-54-9876
(573) 123-4567

Mrs. Doe stated that her husband had gotten mad at her and hit her several times in the face. Mrs. Doe explained that she tried to get away but added that he was holding her by the hair and he was just too strong. Mrs. Doe went on to explain that she finally kneed him in the groin, which is when he let her go. Mrs. Doe continued, stating that she had not done anything to deserve this, and added that when she got away, she locked herself in the bathroom.

At this point Mrs. Doe has made her initial statement but seemed to be leaving portions of the story out. According to what she has told officers so far, the incident was caused for unknown reasons. This particular situation is sensitive, because she may have been involved in a sexual relationship outside the marriage. If this is the case, officers don't want to make her sound like a tramp, turning her off, yet at the same time officers should want to get the entire story. And again, she has corroborated, at least partially, her husband's version of events.

Do her actions outside the relationship justify what her husband has done… no way… but somehow leaving those facts out of the report just doesn't set well with most officers. Officers should report all of the facts, forward the report, and let the chips fall where they may.

The prosecutor needs to know the quality of the witness that he or she will put on the stand, so when the defense tries to discredit them, they are prepared for the worst. In some cases, the prosecutors may handle these situations by introducing these actions during their case in chief, desensitizing the jury early on. In short, it's better coming from them than the defense. If it comes from the defense then there is an inference that the prosecution was being sneaky, underhanded, or was just uninformed. The prosecution needs to be in charge of the entire trial, and if they don't know everything, they can't be in charge; at times they may be found lacking. If that happens… who's to blame?

Side note: While responding to calls of service, some of which involve very attractive people who happen to be in a vulnerable situation… remember, this is not part of a dating game. Officers should not be using this as an opportunity to victimize those who needed help. This may seem obvious, but there's one guarantee… given enough time… officers will witness these events. In those cases, interject yourself, and document…document…document. If by chance the victim makes a formal complaint, an internal investigation will follow. Enough said.

The next step is to have Mrs. Doe sit down and fill out a written statement, which will be transcribed, or summarized, in the narrative; it will also be attached to the report. Really serious statements made by anyone involved should be enclosed in quotation marks.

If officers choose to videotape or digitally record the statement, now is the time, because she may not feel like cooperating later on. Frankly, her statement may be captured on the officer's body worn camera. If a videotaped statement is prepared, ensure that the date, the start and stop times, the location, and all of the people present during the interview are documented. If the footage on body-worn cameras is used, they must have their own legal statement attached with the report to ensure they are admissible in court.

When the statement is completed, the tape should be placed in to evidence, with some notation made in the narrative of the report.

If a digital recording is made, the information is to be transferred to storage media and then placed into evidence. The issues surrounding body-worn cameras will be addressed in a separate section, but there are statements which need to be noted in the body of the report, which may potentially be part of a departmental policy.

Example: *Mrs. Doe agreed to sit down and fill out a written statement about what had happened. The written statement itself read similar to the verbal statement but did add that Mr. Doe had been yelling at her when he went to get the knife. According to Mrs. Doe's statement, Mr. Doe was screaming, "I'm going to kill you." Ms. Doe's statement will be attached to this report.*

When asked, Mrs. Doe agreed to digitally record a statement about what had happened. Present for the recording was Mrs. Doe, Detective Day, and myself (including the start and stop times too). That recording was transferred to a compact disc, which was secured into evidence.

The next step is to collect the evidence… which would be done while Mrs. Doe was filling out a written statement.

Photography: the choices offered at most departments are digital, film, or body-worn camera footage, but whatever your choice, make sure you understand how the equipment works. There is an advantage to using digital images, because there is no guesswork, the picture is either captured… or it isn't. The benefit is that as soon as the image is captured the officer will know whether he or she needs to take the image again. With film cameras several pictures may have to be taken, to ensure "one" good image, changing the settings with each picture in an attempt to capture one image. This technique is called bracketing.

The narrative should include a log of the pictures taken (photo log). Below is an example:

1. *Picture of the victim's face*
2. *Overall picture of the residence.*
3. *Close up of the address on the residence.*
4. *Entrance.*

5. *Knife that is stuck into the wall. Left of the door, as you face the door. Marked as #1.*
6. *Knife lying next to a scale, marked as item number 1.*
7. *Etc....*

Officers should consider the crime itself... not all crimes "merit" ... every one of these steps; that is, time is "always" a consideration. This could be a touchy subject, and departmental policy may dictate if an officer needs to draw a scaled diagram of the scene. If an officer is at the scene of a serious felony... and/or department policy requires a diagram...remember to take the least intrusive steps first; which means pictures are taken before you move or collect the evidence. If a diagram is needed, now is the time, but measuring the evidence for scaled diagrams will be discussed and described later. New officers may find themselves wondering why a scaled diagram is needed, if you have pictures, but those pictures don't provide measurements; so, the diagram augments the pictures by giving them dimension.

The next step is to seize any evidence that the officer feels will assist in the prosecution of Mr. Doe; so, seize the knife. A description of all the evidence seized at the scene should be included in the narrative of the report (or potentially a supplemental report...one officer handles the call for service... and the other handles the evidence).

Example:

1. *Large nine-inch butcher knife.*
2. *Black handle, about four inches in length.*
3. *Removed from a wall in the living-room; left of the front door, as you look outside.*

If the case is serious enough a scaled crime scene diagram should be prepared and attached to the report. Several methods can be used to measure the evidence: Base-line coordinate, or triangulation.

It is not the intention of this book to teach evidence collection, we simply want to provide a report writing format that can be repeated, and applied to city ordinance violations, misdemeanors, felonies, and the start of a traffic crash reconstruction. However, a brief description of each may be needed before we can continue; and there are thousands of departments where they have very few specialists. I suggest that most small departments… specifically in rural areas… are filled by officers who are expected to do a bit of everything; they are the generalists. New recruits are considered generalists. That said, if a diagram is required, officers have two methods for reporting the location of the evidence seized. Again, if pictures are taken, the use of a scaled diagram may not be needed; accident investigation may be the exception to the rule… we mark and record the evidence at the scene of an accident… every time. That said, the process is the same; regardless of whether it's a vehicle's point of final rest, or a knife laying on a kitchen floor. In that case, an officer will use the Baseline Coordinate Method or Triangulation.

In either case, two fixed points are needed to record the location of one piece of evidence; whether that's a knife on the kitchen floor, or the tire on a vehicle. This is done so a crime scene can be recreated in the future. In either case, officers want to ensure the proper location, and/or orientation of said evidence.

Baseline Coordinate Method: If this option is chosen, a tape measure of some type is used to run parallel to the evidence that is to be recorded. It's suggested to use a wall, or some fixed location, to run your baseline. All the measurements start on one side of the tape and extends out depending on the first item's location. Again, each item will receive two measurements, so there is the length down the tape, and then the distance to the right or left of the tape (depending on the orientation of your baseline and evidence).

So, your first measurement may be 5' down the tape, and 3' to the right, using 90 degrees off the baseline. If by chance the officer is trying to measure a large object, and record both the location and orientation, the officer needs to take two more measurements, a location on the other side of the object. These two measurements… two per side… will give the object both its location and orientation.

Triangulation: Triangulation works in a similar fashion, and the officer will need fixed locations to start, with distances to each point. Again, two measurements are needed to record one point, and four measurements are needed to record position and orientation.

Diagram 1… Triangulation… Two Simple Examples

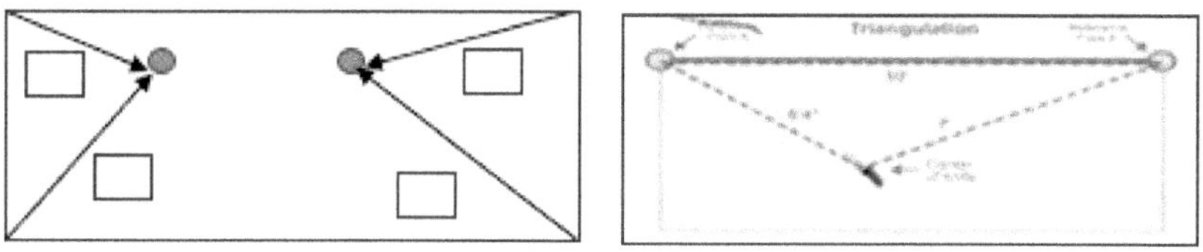

Diagram 2… Baseline Coordinate… Two Simple Examples

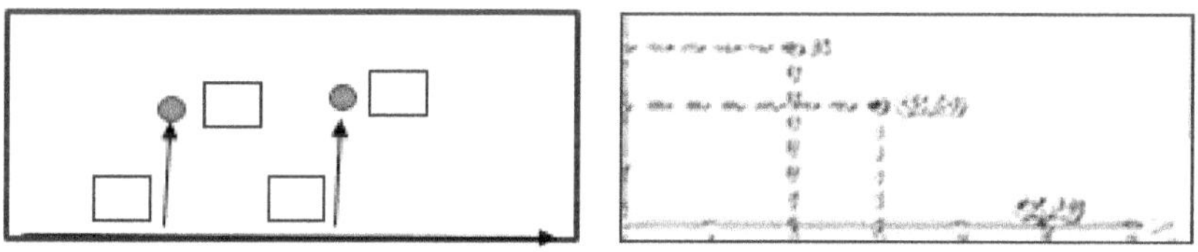

Regardless of the choice officers make, each point they measure to will need to be labeled; so, there is no question what is being measured. Experience suggests baseline is used more often in traffic crashes and triangulation used more often inside crime scenes; although this is not a hard and fast rule. Suggestion: Officers should remember, the diagrams are not necessarily part of the written report we are teaching here; it's a separate form which is attached to the report and referenced in the narrative. We offer the examples just so new officers are aware of how to incorporate the diagrams with a finished report; if the departmental policy requires them. The truth is… not all crimes will justify the amount of time needed to complete these techniques.

This idea would also go along with a list of officers that have entered into a crime scene. If officers are assigned the duty of guarding the doorway to a crime scene and recording who came and went… that's simply a separate list officers will be attached to the report, while referencing the list in the body of the narrative.

Regardless of the officer's crime scene duties… the body of your narrative will be formatted the same way (use the same basic format provided… later).

Keep in mind, that given other crimes, other steps may need to be taken before officers leave the residence. In some cases, an attempt to locate and lift latent prints may be done. In that case, the prints should be photographed (film or digital), included in a log, and then lifted. We suggest that if this is done, a macro lens be used, just in case something happens to the print after it's lifted. In some cases, the print that is captured with a macro lens can still be used to identify suspects. The seized prints will also be included in the list of evidence that was seized.

Another step that may be taken is the area canvass. Sometimes the information that neighbors have can assist in the investigation and also the prosecution of the offender. This information can be recorded either in the main body of the report narrative, or in a separate supplemental report. Either method is acceptable but may be governed according to departmental policy.

Conclusion

The conclusion is the final part of the report and simply explains what has happened to both the victim and offender. The prosecutors are going to want to know what happened to the victim: Were they hospitalized; did they go to a shelter; and do they wish to pursue charges against the offender. In addition, the prosecutors will want to know the status of the offender: Any statements that he made; when the statements were made; and did Miranda apply. Furthermore, a detailed explanation of the offender's criminal history should be listed in this section of the report. This last bit of information may not be admitted during the first part of the trial (there are exceptions…to prove a pattern or Motus Operandi… for a series of criminal behavior), but it may steel the prosecutor's resolve, and it will be admitted during the sentencing phase of the trial. Moreover, some departments may require a sworn statement section, and the exact verbiage will be dictated by departmental policy. This is also the section where statements involving the footage from body worn cameras are listed, and again the exact verbiage will be dictated by departmental policy.

Example: *Before leaving, Mrs. Doe stated that her head hurt. The ambulance crew had already arrived and started to assess her. Mrs. Doe decided that she wanted to go to the hospital and was transported to the St. John's Medical Center by ambulance for treatment. Before leaving, Mrs. Doe agreed to have a copy of her medical records dropped off at the sheriff's office. Copies of those records will be attached to this report. It is also my understanding that Mrs. Doe is going to make application for an Ex Parte; having been given instructions on the application process.*

Mr. Doe was arrested for 2nd degree domestic violence and transported to the sheriff's office for booking. Upon arrival at the jail the handcuffs were removed, and the booking process was completed.

During the booking process Mr. Doe was informed of his Miranda Rights, per a departmental form, which he stated he understood.

Mr. Doe signed the form, waiving his rights.

When asked, Mr. Doe agreed to fill out a written statement, which will be attached to this report. Mr. Doe's statement read very similar to his original statement(s). In the written statement Mr. Doe claimed that he was "very sorry, nobody deserves to be hurt like that." Mr. Doe was incarcerated, pending the application of an arrest warrant.

The dispatcher provided me with a copy of Mr. Doe's criminal history, which was attached to this report and detailed the following:

Ten felonies, with one conviction; five misdemeanors, with two convictions; and two ordinance violations, with no convictions. The history contained charges such as: Burglary 1st, stealing, possession of a controlled substance, assault, and three counts of domestic assault third.

All evidence was submitted, per departmental policy.

This report is intended to be a summary of events. It may contain paraphrased conversations and may not be in the exact sequence of events. For any exact quotes and for specific sequence of events, please refer to my body-worn camera recording, which was activated at the time of the incident.

I certify under the penalty of perjury under the laws of the State (whatever State you work) that all statements made herein are true and accurate and that I am entering my authorized user ID and password to authenticate it.

A copy of this report will be forwarded to the prosecutor's office for their review and possible action.

I have nothing further to report at this time.

Respectfully Submitted.

Deputy Aaron J. Pinson, MA

Completed Report... Minus Attachments

On December 17th, 2005 at approximately 12:30 PM Detective Day and I were "summoned" to 12345 South Highway 63 Rolla, MO in reference to a domestic disturbance. Dispatch explained that a female had called them and reported that her husband had hit her, adding that the caller was now locked in the bathroom. While on the way to the scene we were informed, by radio, that the caller claimed that her husband had a knife, and had been chasing her with it before she locked the door to the bathroom. Dispatch went on to explain, that there was a violent history at this residence, adding that the husband has been arrested three times; each time for domestic assault. Dispatch continued, and stated that the caller had not hung up the phone, and that they could still hear a lot of yelling in the background.

Upon arrival at the scene, just moments in front of Detective Day, I observed a white male standing in the front yard of the residence; he was wearing nothing but "heart" covered boxers. As I got out, I noticed that the male had what appeared to be red scratches all over his chest, he was breathing heavy, and his face was red and blotchy; he appeared very angry. I could clearly see that the man had nothing in his hands, and after he turned around, he walked towards me.

The male was identified as:

John W. Doe
DOB: 01-01-79
SSN: 123-45-6789
(573) 123-4567

Mr. Doe stated that he was tired of that "bitch", and added that he was going to divorce "her sorry ass." When asked, Mr. Doe stated that he had found a letter in his wife's coat pocket, and added that for the last few weeks she has been having an affair. Mr. Doe explained that after he read the letter, he "just lost it", grabbing her off the couch by her hair. Mr. Doe went on, stating that he couldn't seem to stop himself, adding that he hit her three or four times in the face, which is when she kneed him in the "balls." Mr. Doe continued, stating that she ran into the bathroom and locked the door.

When asked, Mr. Doe stated that his wife never raised a hand to him, adding that he never really gave her a chance. Mr. Doe explained that the scratches on his chest were done when she was trying to wiggle out of his grasp, adding that the only reason he let go was because "the bitch kneed him in the balls." When asked, Mr. Doe admitted that he had picked up a kitchen knife but had quickly decided that she was not worth it. Mr. Doe claimed that he had stuck the knife in the living-room wall before walking outside.

At this point, Mr. Doe was detained in double-locked handcuffs, and placed into the rear of my patrol car, pending the outcome of the investigation. Once Mr. Doe was secured in the back of my patrol car we attempted to locate the victim. The front door to the residence was open, and after I announced our arrival, we waited a few moments before entering their home. When nobody answered or came to the door we entered the residence, noting that the entire living-room was in disarray. The pillows for the couch were on the floor, an end-table was lying on its side, pictures had been knocked off the wall, and there was a large knife stuck in the wall near the front door.

There was a hallway that ran to the left of the living-room, and we continued to yell as we made our way down the hall. A short time later a female opened the door at the end of the hall and stated that her husband had hit her. The female's right eye was almost completely closed, the results of bruising and swelling. The bruising ranged in color from dark purple to pink. In addition, her nose looked out of place, as if it was swelling on one side. Furthermore, I noticed that her top lip was bruised and swollen; with the same color scheme described above.

The female was identified as:

Jane M. Doe
DOB: 12-12-78
SSN: 321-54-9876
(573) 123-4567

Mrs. Doe stated that her husband had gotten mad at her and hit her several times in the face. Mrs. Doe explained that she tried to get away but added that he was holding her by her hair, and he is just too strong. Mrs. Doe went on to explain that she finally kneed him in the groin, which is when he let her go. Mrs. Doe continued, stating that she had done nothing to deserve this, and added that when she got away, she locked herself in the bathroom.

Mrs. Doe agreed to sit down and fill out a written statement about what had happened. The written statement itself read similar to the verbal statement but did add that Mr. Doe had been yelling at her when he went to get the knife. According to Mrs. Doe's statement, Mr. Doe was screaming, "I'm going to kill you." Mrs. Doe's statement will be attached to this report.

When asked, Mrs. Doe agreed to digitally record a statement about what had happened. Present for the recording was Mrs. Doe, Detective Day, and Myself. That recording was transferred to a compact disc, which was secured into evidence.

The following digital images were taken, transferred to compact disc, and placed into evidence.

1. Overall picture of the residence.
2. Close up of the address on the residence.
3. Entrance.
4. Knife that is stuck into the wall. Left of the door, as you face the door. Marked as #1.
5. Knife lying next to a scale, marked as item number 1.

The following evidence was seized and later placed into an evidence locker.

1. Large nine-inch butcher knife.
    a. Black handle, about four inches in length.
    b. Removed from a wall in the living-room; left of the front door, as you look outside.

Before leaving Mrs. Doe stated that her head hurt. The ambulance crew had already arrived and started to assess her. Mrs. Doe decided that she wanted to go to the hospital and was transported to the St. John's Medical Center by ambulance for treatment. Before leaving, Mrs. Doe agreed to have a copy of her medical records dropped off at the sheriff's office. Copies of those records will be attached to this report. It is also my understanding that Mrs. Doe is going to make application for an Ex Parte; having been given instructions on the application process.

Mr. Doe was arrested for 2nd degree domestic violence, and transported to the sheriff's office for booking. Upon arrival at the jail the handcuffs were removed, and the booking process was completed. During the booking process Mr. Doe was informed of his Miranda Rights, per a departmental form, which he stated he understood. Mr. Doe signed the form, waiving his rights.

When asked, Mr. Doe agreed to fill out a written statement, which will be attached to this report. Mr. Doe's statement read very similar to his original story. In the written statement Mr. Doe claimed that he was "very sorry, nobody deserves to be hurt like that." Mr. Doe was incarcerated, pending the application of an arrest warrant.

The dispatcher provided me with a copy of Mr. Doe's criminal history, which will be attached to this report. The history detailed the following: Ten felonies, with one conviction; five misdemeanors, with two convictions; and two ordinance violations, with no convictions.

The history contained charges such as: Burglary 1st, stealing, possession of a controlled substance, assault, and three counts of domestic assault third.

All evidence seized was submitted into evidence per departmental policy.

This report is intended to be a summary of events. It may contain paraphrased conversations, and may not be in the exact sequence of events. For any exact quotes and for specific sequence of events, please refer to my body-worn camera recording, which was activated at the time of the incident.

I certify under the penalty of perjury under the laws of the State (whatever State you work) that all statements made herein are true and accurate and that I am entering my authorized user ID and password to authenticate it.

A copy of this report will be forwarded to the prosecutor's office for their review and possible action.

I have nothing further to report at this time.

Respectfully Submitted,

Deputy A.J. Pinson, MA

Detective J. Day, BA

Forward to a Police Report

Some agencies require officers to include a synopsis or forward for the police report. If that is the case, the forward is the first paragraph of the police report. It provides the reader with basic information; it provides insight for what is to come.

The forward, or a synopsis, of the report that we have used would read something like this:

On December 17, 2005, at approximately 12:30 PM, officers responded to the 12000 block of So. Highway 63 for a report of domestic violence. John Doe, a white make, of Rolla, MO, was arrested for 2nd degree assault and incarcerated pending warrant application/bond.

This paragraph can also be used to report specific information to the media. In short, this is not a requirement, but an option.

Departmental policy should dictate if this is included in your report or if it's added to another data base.

Probable Cause Statement... Just the Facts

The probable cause statements may be a source of resentment in the law enforcement community. Experienced officers have said many times that "it should be the Prosecutor's job" to fill out that statement. However, the fact is the person that is most familiar with the case should be filling out the statement; ensuring that all of the facts are accurate, and that nothing is misunderstood. This is really a simple document to fill out, and in most cases a standard form can be used.

From a prosecutor's point of view, the entire case should not be detailed in the probable cause statement; that's for the report. The probable cause statement is in this way a synopsis of the report; detailing "only enough" information to get the warrant issued. This is important for two reasons. First, once the prosecutors file the probable cause statement it becomes "public record", and anyone can get access to it through the Freedom of Information Act. Once that happens, the case will be smeared in large print all over the community; thanks in large part to our media, who are in a never-ending search for dirt. This could potentially damage the jury pool, and lead to a change in venue; this would in fact increase the cost of a trial. The second is a strategic philosophy; why provide the defense with information that they are not entitled to have…at that moment. This is not to say that they won't ever get the information, they will, just not at the preliminary hearing. At the preliminary hearing the defense gets a copy of the probable cause statement, and that's it. The tactic is that the defense has no idea what the prosecutor's strategy will be at trial; they can only assume that there is more, and there should be more.

The probable cause statement will be the document that will be forwarded to the judge, who will decide whether an arrest is needed, justified, and constitutional. The judge will base his or her opinion on the facts in the statement, ensuring that all the elements of each crime are met, and that there is indeed probable cause to believe that the suspect has committed the crime. In addition, the judge will decide whether anybody's constitutional rights were violated or will be by the subsequent arrest.

The 4th Amendment of our constitution is very clear, stating "The right of the people to be secure in their persons, houses, papers, and effects, against unreasonable searches and seizures, shall not be violated, and no warrants shall issue, but upon probable cause, supported by Oath or affirmation, and particularly describing the place to be searched, and the persons or things to be seized." The goal is not to delve deeply into the Constitutional aspect of law enforcement because everyone has his or her opinion, and this text is about report writing. The 4th Amendment of the Constitution, printed above, outlines what law enforcement officers have to do in order to obtain a warrant.

The probable cause affidavit, as it is called in Missouri, outlines the probable cause for the arrest and when presented to the prosecutor allows them to obtain warrants from a judge. The probable cause affidavit should be as close to one page as possible and should detail the "highlights" of the report, including all the requirements for the offense charged. In the example case of domestic violence, John W. Doe was arrested and charged with domestic assault 2nd degree.

In the case of 2nd degree domestic assault (Missouri Law), the stature reads, and the prosecutors must prove the following:

Missouri Statute: 565.073. 1. A person commits the offense of domestic assault in the second degree if the act involves a domestic victim, as the term "domestic victim" is defined under section 565.002, and he or she:

(1) Knowingly causes physical injury to such domestic victim by any means, including but not limited to, use of a deadly weapon or dangerous instrument, or by choking or strangulation, or

(2) Recklessly causes serious physical injury to such domestic victim; or

(3) Recklessly causes physical injury to such domestic victim by means of any deadly weapon.

(The offense of domestic assault in the second is a class D felony.)

The first thing that has to be documented for this charge is their relationship. Under the Missouri statute the victim and suspect must be related or residing together or involved in a continuing relationship. Since Jane and John are married and residing together that is pretty easy to prove. The second and final proof required is that John W. Doe knowingly or recklessly caused serious physical injury to Jane M. Doe. In our example, John W. Doe read the note found in his wife's pocket and made a decision to assault her. He then went into the room where she was at, grabbed her by the hair and began punching her in the face. Based upon the physical examination of the victim, made at the scene, it was obvious that he was not "play fighting" with his wife, he intended to do harm to her.

PROBABLE CAUSE STATEMENT

I, Deputy John M. Day, knowing that false statements on this form are punishable by law, state that the facts contained herein were truly observed by me.

1. I have probable cause to believe that John William Doe, DOB: 01-01-1979, SSN: 123-45-6789, OCN: NA, who lives at 12345 South Highway 63 Rolla, Missouri, did, on or about the 17th day of December 2005, commit one or more criminal offenses.
2. The facts supporting this belief are as follows:
   - On December 17, 2005, at approximately 12:30 PM Deputies were summoned to the above address, which is in Phelps County, Missouri, due to a report of a domestic disturbance.

- Mr. Doe informed us that his wife has been having an affair, and that he had struck her three or four times in the face.
- The victim, Jane Mary Doe, explained she had been seated on their couch when her husband attacked her; holding her by the hair and punching her in the face. She was able to break free from him by striking him in the groin. She then fled further into the residence where she barricaded herself in the bathroom.
- Jane Doe was transported to the Hospital for treatment of her injuries, which were later discovered to be a severe fracture of the left cheekbone.
  - **a.** I believe that the defendant will not appear in court in response to a criminal summons because: The suspect in this matter has an extensive record of failure to appear warrants being issued. Based upon his past history it is likely that he will not appear regarding this offense.
  - b. I believe that the defendant poses:

1. A danger to a crime victim because: The suspect has shown a tremendous lack of control regarding his emotions and severely beat his wife. It is likely that he will do so again given the current circumstances.
2. A danger to the community of to any other person because: N/A
   - The defendant was arrested on Thursday, December 17th, 2005 at approximately 12:40 P.M
   - Referring Department Phelps County Sheriff Office, Report Number 05-00 1234

Print Name: John M. Day, Detective

Signature: *John M. Day*

Date: Wednesday, March 11, 2026

The probable cause statement contains some of the same information as the report, but only focuses on some of the facts, and does not explain how the law enforcement officer came by those facts. The date, time, and jurisdiction are important and are the facts that open up the statement. The court must know when the crime occurred, and that they do in fact have jurisdiction in the case. Next, a brief description of the crime is listed, making sure to detail all of the elements of that specific crime, without listing that crime on the statement. The reason for this is simple; the prosecutors may decide that the crime needs to be charged differently. They will be hard pressed to do that if the officer has listed the charge on the statement itself.

Report Outline... Building Blocks

The outline described below is both general and fluid, so it can be applied to almost any situation: City ordinance violations; misdemeanors; felonies; and violations of U.S. Code. The outline can be used as the basis for more ordinary calls such as property damage, assaults, and stealing to the more complicated investigations such as accident reconstruction or a homicide.

In cases where the investigation is more complicated, one must just add those sections where they fit in. In addition, this format can be used for both the preliminary investigations, and the follow-ups which are almost certainly going to happen (Original response or supplementals).

1. **Preliminary section.**
    - Date.
    - Time.
    - Location of the call.
    - Reason for the response.
    - Supplemental information

2. **Upon arrival.**
    - Who was contacted?
    - Evidence at the scene (what was observed).
    - Victim's condition (if applicable).
    - Condition of the area (if applicable).
    - Observations! What did you hear, see, smell, etc…
3. **Statements.**
    - Victim's allegations.
    - Suspect's defense.
    - Witness's observations.
4. **After arrival.**
    - Search for suspect.
    - Collection of evidence
        - Itemized list (who found it, and the location).
        - What was done with the evidence?
    - Photographs.
        - Photo log.
    - Crime scene diagram.
        - Base-line coordinate method.
        - Triangulation.
    - Complete list of stolen or damaged property.
    - Fingerprints.
        - Where were they located?
    - Area Canvass.
        - Who was contacted, and what did they have to offer the investigation.
5. **Conclusion.**
    - Victim.
        - Hospital treatment, shelter, etc…
    - Suspect.
        - Arrest (detailed).
        - Criminal history.
        - Miranda and statements after the arrest.

REPORT OUTLINE

POLICE
PINSON
808

PART TWO: Police Report Writing Other Aspects

Who, What, When, Where, Why, and How

Everyone is going to want the answers to these questions: Who did it; what happened; what are the mitigating circumstances; when did the alleged crime occur; where did the crime occur; why was the crime committed, and what was the motivation; and how was the crime committed. Take a moment and try and address each and every one of these questions, but keep in mind you may not be able to answer them all. There is no such thing as a perfect case; each case has its strengths and weaknesses.

Who

This will probably be one of the easier elements to determine; especially if the officers are responding to a domestic. However, investigations can be more complex; there are many unsolved crimes. In the end, officers need to be arresting the right person, and again, asking clarifying questions at the scene can help with this. Unfortunately, tracking down the right person may take more investigation, and that is beyond the scope of this book. What's important to note at this point is the need to document everything.

What

This is important because it identifies the crimes the suspect will be accused, and the elements of the crimes that have to be proven…before an arrest can be made, and later at trial. Without getting too deep into the weeds, every crime has elements… or facts… that need to be met before a crime can be charged. These elements can be found in city ordinance violations, county, state statutes, and/or United States Code.

This obligation initially falls on the individual officers; so often new recruits, or probationary officers, have a state statute book with them; these books list all of the state statutes… each with their own set of elements, and as time goes on, their education, training, and experience will grow, and their familiarity with these elements solidifies.

When

The date and time are essential, for a number of reasons. However, it dictates which laws are going to be proven during court trials…or the elements of the crimes charged. Said differently, if it is discovered that the crime had been committed years prior…the laws may have been different…and therefore, the elements may have been different. So, the date and time is more critical than it initially suggests.

Law enforcement officers need to separate…at some point…the differences in the date and time of their response…opposed to…the date and time the victim claims said the crime occurred. Moreover, most crimes have a statute of limitations, and while this may not directly affect the report, it will be important for the prosecutor, defense attorney, and judge.

Where

This element specifically addresses the jurisdiction of the court, but it can be more complex, because of specific geographic boundaries, and the location of a crime (vehicle pursuit initiated in one jurisdiction and an arrest in another jurisdiction…with multiple violations in both). Example: A city that is divided into multiple counties, such as Sullivan or Pacific, Missouri. This can be especially apparent in a drug arrest that was affected in one county, by a municipal officer, but was initiated by a traffic violation in a different county. The entire drug case may hinge, in part or in whole, on the outcome of the traffic violation(s).

Both prosecutors need to be involved and they need to communicate with the department, and each other.

However, the circumstances behind the traffic stop must be spelled out, and easily understood, so prosecutors can apply their actions and decisions to the case(s). Moreover, there is still the issue of probable cause statements...will there be just one...or will there be two?

The answers should be found in department policy or agreements with both prosecutors' offices.

Why

Intent is a requirement for violating most criminal statutes; however, there are exceptions. Either way, the investigating officer needs to document the intent in their report... if known. The two principles that make up "intent" are Mens Rea, which basically means a guilty mind, and Actus Reus, which basically means the guilty act. These are Latin terms which essentially mean that the suspect thought about the crime, and then acted on his thoughts; put together they go to prove that the suspect wanted to commit the act in question.

An exception might be a crime that simply requires the suspect's careless disregard of someone else's safety. Said differently, they didn't mean to hurt anybody, but what they did was so incredibly irre sponsible, and their actions led to the injury or death of the victim.

Moreover, the courts will apply a "reasonable man" concept to each case...which means, would a reasonable man believe that the outcome of the events be a reasonable expectation or inference. An example might be a motor vehicle crash, where the driver of one of the vehicles is impaired by drugs or alcohol, and someone was hurt in the accident: Passenger, pedestrian, or another driver. So, is injury and death a reasonable expectation if someone was to drink and drive? The offender's intentions really have no bearing on the final outcome, because the results are a reasonable expectation; driving drunk is inherently dangerous... with obvious risks to motoring public and pedestrians.

Proving intent might be problematic, but an investigator really has two options: Incriminating statements, and a history of their actions. Example, a suspect may confess that he or she intended to commit the crime, simplifying matters for the investigator. In one case, a suspect confessed three times that he was going to rape a stranded motorist on the side of the road: Once in a verbal statement; once in a written statement; and once in digitally recorded video. The victim was an off-duty nurse and her five-year-old son was with her at the time. The last thing he wrote on his statement, and admitted on the video, was that he was going to "rape her right there." In that case, the suspect went to prison for attempted rape.

The irony was the defense attorney involved, was the first attorney to depose one of the authors of this book; and in so doing, schooled him for future testimony. The same defense attorney represented the offender described above, and it was the same author's last court case (testimony)… and the suspect went to prison.

The author, who had been involved in this case, could not be more grateful for that initial lesson; even though it was… embarrassing.

Another way to prove intent is by considering all of the suspect's actions leading up to the crime; those substantial steps. In the case described above the suspect had taken several steps to further his crime: He pulled his vehicle behind the victim's parked car (which had run out of fuel, leaving the victim's stranded), so close it made her uncomfortable; he tried to force the victim into his vehicle; he ripped her blouse open; he tried to kiss her; and he fled the scene before police arrived.

The confessions were the icing on the cake. Everything, in this case, was documented as described above… and the offender was arrested, tried, convicted, and sentenced to prison (first offense); intent was never really questioned. However, his… intelligence… was considered as a mitigating factor.

How…What's the Suspects Modus Operandi

Answering this question can really help you prove that the right person was arrested and is sitting in front of the jury. This is especially true if he or she divulges certain specifics about the crime, during an interrogation. This can be addressed if the interrogator asks clarifying question, and it can eliminate those that are trying to take credit for a crime they did not commit. As an example, during the interrogation, the suspect confesses that he used a belt to strangle a victim who was shot to death; suggesting that this was a false confession.

Or the suspect might confess that he took something personal from the victim… a trophy. In short, it's something that only the offender could have known, and a fact that will ensure his or her conviction.

But… the investigator must include it in his or her report.

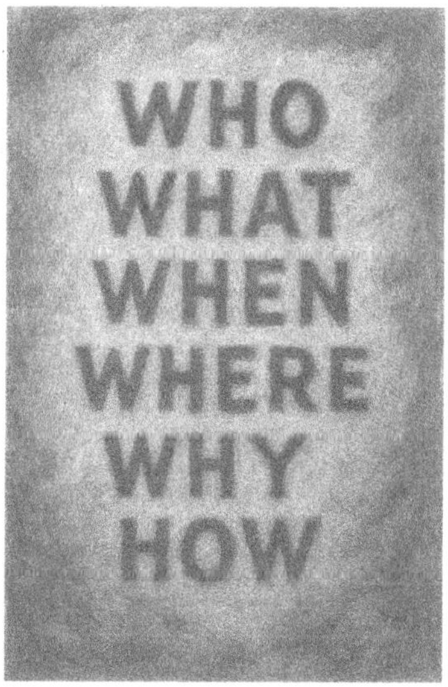

Miranda

This is the greatest country in the world, and some of those benefits "require" the government to inform its citizens of their constitutional rights; Amen. The authors are not sure of any other country that has these protections or is responsible for informing its citizens of those protections, when its citizens are at their most vulnerable.

The police are obligated to inform, those who are in custody, and being questioned about violations of city ordinances, state statutes or U.S. Code… of these protections; but Miranda does not cover all questions…there are exceptions.

Moreover, the United States Supreme court ruled that it was possible to violate the "spirit" of the law (due to a case in Rolla, MO). In the case described the conviction was overturned.

Point of interest: A suspect was arrested for a crime in Rolla, MO. The detective had been trained to interrogate suspects using a specific strategy. The overarching strategy was to get a confession, from the arrested suspect, after Miranda was given and understood. However, the tactics used to get said confession was the point of contention for the US Supreme Court.

The tactic used required the detective to speak with the suspect…about the crime, and before Miranda… in an effort to grease the wheels. The idea stemmed from a fear that the Miranda Warning would steal the suspect's opposition or resistance.

Whereas, speaking to the suspect… initially… in a casual conversation, would spur future cooperation.

So once the suspect had confessed, the detective would "then" inform the suspect of his Miranda Rights… which he understood… and the "official" interrogation started. The only statements included in the report were those given "after" the Miranda Warning had been given and understood. This case eventually led to the United States Supreme Court; and the court ruled that the detective involved had violated the "spirit" of the law.

The Miranda Warning does not cover questions which involve the suspect's name, date of birth, or phone number, although people can still refuse to answer. If that happens… the government… will often get a "John Doe" warrant on the suspect… and the suspect, would remain in jail until they provided the identifiable information.

Moreover, the Miranda Warning does not apply to questions where "exigent" circumstances apply; but often… the courts will rule on these issues… right before the trial, during the trial, or on appeal.

The nature of evidence gained under exigent circumstances, is that law enforcement will not know if the evidence will be admissible… until a judge decides. The nature of evidence gained under exigent circumstances, is that law enforcement will not know if the evidence will be admissible… until a judge decides.

Exigent circumstances simply means that law enforcement did not have the time to inform the suspect of these protections; often it has to do with the preservation of life… or evidence. Said differently, if there is a chance someone might suffer significant injury or death or the loss of evidence… these warnings "may" not be needed; but departmental policy will probably be very conservative on this issue.

For these reasons, members of law enforcement make these decisions… very conservatively. So…if in doubt…inform the suspects of their Miranda Rights. Normally law enforcement agencies use Miranda Cards and Miranda Forms; which limit mistakes, and most defense attorneys will challenge this aspect of a confession.

The Miranda Forms provide an advantage, because there is a place for the suspect to sign… indicating they understand. If an officer does not use a card, or a form, there is a real chance that the courts could exclude the evidence which followed, because the officer may stumble during their testimony.

There are often very conservative strategies to Miranda, and while not required, some individual officers will use the Miranda Warning, when asking guilt seeking questions to suspects who are "not" in custody. This removes a defense attorney's argument that their client (suspect) was not free to leave...when the suspect was being questioned. If the court rules in the defense's favor…law enforcement…loses the evidence gained during and after questioning. For these reasons, law enforcement agencies, have adopted these very conservative law enforcement strategies.

So, follow your individual department's policies in the Miranda Warning; officers should document the date and time the suspect was advised of these rights. By being aware of the pitfalls and using these strategies, law enforcement professionals ensure the evidence seized after questioning, is admissible in a criminal court.

This book was not intended to be a class on evidence, so a decision was made to keep this brief. However, the basics needed to be included, so we can document this process in writing. If a serious felony has been committed, the "initial" report itself will probably end before an interrogation begins: Initial report; supplemental reports involving detectives; and suspect's arrests and interrogation. In those cases…the same report format…will be used during the interrogation, and in all the supplemental reports. That said, the initial reports, and all of the supplemental reports, use the same format we have provided.

Hearsay

This is always an issue of debate amongst officers; that is, what to include in a report, and what to leave out. Frankly, officers' decisions are going to be based on a number of issues: Department policy; officer experience; common sense; and street smarts. And finally, whatever your supervisor tells you to take out or include.

Regardless, if a written report has hearsay evidence included… when the case goes to court… the evidence is simply excluded; so, there is no real reason to exclude it from the report (except the argument that's the way we have always done it). It could be argued to report all of this evidence, because there are so many exceptions that it's hard to stay current. So, if the evidence is not reported, then the argument for an exception simply can't be made; and potentially admissible evidence is not disclosed to a judge or jury. Generally officers repeat that they only include the facts in a police report...nothing more, and nothing less. Again, that's only partially true...or true only part of the time.

A criminal investigation should include all of the evidence in the report; hearsay and all. With one caveat, officers need to balance the information that they are including in their report with common sense. We don't suggest you include a statement from someone, who heard something from a friend, who overheard two people talking... etc....

This reasoning is based on the hearsay law, which changes every year. Someone could probably argue that more hearsay evidence is admitted into court, based on exceptions, than evidence which is excluded. We are police officers, and not attorneys. The police can't be expected to stay current on all the hearsay updates, while attorneys can.

So put it in the report, and let the attorneys worry about what is, and what is not, admissible into court. Moreover, no harm comes from simply documenting hearsay evidence that will probably never see the inside of a courtroom. The prosecutor will present his or her case in chief, first. If there is hearsay evidence included in the report, then prosecutor will never bring it up; that is, if he doesn't think he can get it admitted.

The last thing the defense is going to do is bring up inadmissible hearsay evidence that is documented in a police report, mums the word of the day. In short, no harm no foul.

The last point, and arguably the most important, is the evidence itself. If the officer does not document the evidence, then prosecutors will never be allowed to evaluate its merits.

Unfortunately, that evidence will never see the inside of a courtroom and may have been the final nudge the jury needed to reach a "guilty" verdict. If that happens… did the victims receive justice?

Opinion

Generally, officers should remember that nobody wants to know their personal opinions, although they may find themselves in situations where they want to share them; the newer the officer, the stronger that statement is. However, this is not a hard and fast rule. There may be times where an officer's personal opinion is both needed and required. Honestly, that's what experts testify about…their opinions.

As an officer's career progresses, and their experience increases, they may be sent to training which makes them an expert, in very specific areas of study. Over a period of time, they may become an expert in some field, such as traffic crash reconstruction. So, when acting in that capacity, including opinions in the report may be allowed. However, outside of that specific instance, officers should keep their personal opinions out of a report. Enough said.

Lingo, Generic Description or Words, and Abbreviations

Any technical field has its own way of describing different terms used in their industry. I suggest that the United States Military are prone to this issue; they use acronyms for everything but pronounce them as if they were written words. An example of this is, "The United States Military Police School," and the acronym for that is, U.S.M.P.S.; but they pronounce it as if it's a word…like USAMPS.

This issue is fine for the professions who are directly involved; and law enforcement has their own language. Unfortunately, a significant portion of society is not, or will not, be familiar with the terminology; so, those that choose to use this when speaking to the public…might as well be speaking a foreign language.

For these reasons, when law enforcement professionals are drafting reports that will become available to the public, they should "not" use this type of verbiage. The goal of this book was not intended to teach law enforcement professionals how to read or write the English language. In contrast, the goal is to offer a report writing format, which can be used over-and-over again; eventually becoming like… muscle memory.

There is an expectation when law enforcement professionals are hired… anywhere… and departments everywhere expect you to understand the English language. Normally people are better off using the format and to write… like they speak… but don't use this specific type of language; even if that's how you really talk. Example: Don't use law enforcement's "10-code" to describe certain actions in your police report; because most of the public won't understand. Generally speaking, the code for back in service is 10-8; but if that's what you write in your report… you will confuse the hell out of people who are not affiliated with law enforcement.

The police report should be clear and understood, by most people, and if you write in a way that is confusing people… your cases will never see the inside of a court room. Said differently, the victims of crime want and expect a certain amount of responsibility, accountability, and justice; unfortunately, reports that are confusing… helps serve nobody. So… don't use this type of language in your report.

Case or Time Management

For new officers time can be a real challenge. As calls come in, and reports stack up, the panic can set in. This feeling of being overwhelmed can be debilitating, and your focus may be distracted. A simple solution is, take a report, and write the report. You may find that more investigation is needed, but get your initial report completed; you can always write supplements using the same format.

Unfortunately, when it rains it pours, and officers will not always have the luxury of immediately writing their reports. Moreover, young enthusiastic officers want to do as much as they can, as fast as they can, so again reports can stack up. Before an officer realizes he has a number of reports that haven't been written, and there is an unhappy supervisor breathing down their necks.

Time Lines

Keeping track of the times that certain things happen is absolutely critical for a case. It can be devastating in a court room. Often an organization will have a computer application that can help the police officer log the times: Time that a dispatcher will give you a call; the time that you arrived at the scene; times when others arrive at the scene; document the length of a traffic stop, or the amount of time you were on the scene before requesting an ambulance; and what time you went back into service. Loosing track of these times can be catastrophic to a case. Defense attorneys can use it, along with smoke and mirrors, to suggest… just about anything.

In addition, it may be years before the case actually goes to trial, and while the times may be fresh in your mind a few days later, they will be all but forgotten on the day of trial. You may find it helpful to include these times in your report. This prevents having to bring other documentation with you, and it may be easier to understand if you have incorporated the times in your report.

Example: Two deputies were dispatched to a section of interstate to assist two troopers who were fighting with an angry, and drugged, pedestrian. In addition to walking down the side of the interstate, he had a warrant for his arrest. The deputies responded to the scene from a town which was approximately seven miles northeast of their location. The troopers were on the eastbound side, and as the deputies arrived on the westbound side, they advised the dispatchers of their arrival. Unfortunately, this would only add to the confusion a few years later.

The deputies had technically arrived, but because of the interstate's design, they had to continue westbound for a stretch, turn around, and approach the scene for a second time. The pedestrian would later die, due to excited delirium, which is a drugged condition. The question to be answered later in court, was how long had the deputies actually been at the scene before an ambulance was called? Honestly, questions could have been avoided by preparing a better written police report.

The lesson to be learned... document... document... document.

Evidence

There is no real secret to collecting evidence. Nor are there any hard and fast rules that govern the way an officer approaches the collection of the evidence. However, when you are collecting evidence remember to do the least intrusive methods first, because once started, you can't start over; so, start with a walkthrough to secure the scene...pictures...and then more intrusive steps that might have a larger effect. But a word of caution...once a piece of evidence is moved...it will never be in the exact same position again. The one exception to this might be in your individual department's policies and procedures. These may list a process that all officers in that department must follow. However, having some procedure that you use consistently will increase the odds of getting your evidence submitted. In short, it will make you more efficient and effective.

The Army's Criminal Investigative Unit has a list of steps that they use to collect evidence. Frankly, it's a proven process, so we have included it. However there are other procedures that you could use; this is just one process, but again it's a proven process.

One on the most important fundamentals to remember is, you only get one chance to do this right. So take your least intrusive steps first, and then move on to the next step.

Another challenge to crime scenes is the desire for everyone to see it, before you have had a chance to work it. For example, you might find the Chief trying to do a walk through a residence of a recent murder. While your average road officer can't prevent his or her chief from making this mistake, there are a few things that you can do to discourage the practice. Start by making a list of everyone that enters and exits the crime scene; include the date and time of their entrance and exit. Attach the list to your report, which will eventually find its way into the hands of a skilled defense attorney.

Anyone on the list will probably be served with a subpoena to appear in court and forced to answer a few difficult questions. Normally, this will prevent the unwanted "lookie-loos" that are curious about the crime scene. Problem solved.

Body Worn Cameras

Body Worn Cameras have already integrated in to modern policing; protecting both the officer and the citizens they are paid to protect. Initially law enforcement resisted the idea, but over time it has proven its potential and worth.

It's now possible for a Chief of Police to be on vacation… in Hawaii… and to monitor the tense negotiations between a barricaded offender and his officers. If citizens complain about a police encounter they can come to the police department, and officials can screen the encounter together; potentially leading to an internal investigation or the disqualification of the complaint.

The next generation of body-worn cameras will be integrated with Artificial Intelligence. The addition of AI will stack the deck in favor of the individual officers and increase their odds of survival.

An officer's gear can now detect whether an officer has been stabbed or shot, and thereby dispatching additional units and medical support. The AI also integrates facial recognition; allowing authorities to track where the offender came, and where the offender ran.

Body worn cameras operate as a series of checks and balances, because the law enforcement officer knows he is being recorded. However, the camera system also protects the officer by demonstrating that their persona actions were justified. In the case of an officer involved shooting, or an in-custody death, the body worn cameras have become an integrated part of an officer's gear.

Artificial Intelligence

Artificial Intelligence is already being tested in limited locations around the United States; so the question as to its involvement is no longer up for debate… it's here. However, it still represents some challenges as to how its incorporated into individual cities. Moreover, not all citizens agree with its implementation. Some cities are testing AI, and have already linked it into their 911 systems.

In one specific location the city owns 400 camera systems, which are placed on the city streets. The community has an additional 150 cameras, but the AI has linked them together, using them to monitor sections of the metropolitan areas.

The camera systems function as Law Enforcements "Black Box," and after an incident has happened, they can use the system to track offenders. In some cases law enforcement officers gear are equipped with a technology which detects if the officers have been stabbed or shot; immediately activating their body worn cameras. Once the cameras are activated the offender can be identified with facial recognition; and their individual path can be tracked...both where they came from and where they are going. The next generation of body worn camera systems are reported to have AI already equipped.

Challenges to AI in law enforcement focus on the balance between security and/or the monitoring of the citizenry. People of color justify this argument because there is already a history of over policing in minority areas. The citizens do not want to become victims of crime, but they do not want city officials monitoring their every move...without justification.

City AI is also incorporating drones into the camera systems already described, and often, the 911 system can have eyes on a crime scene before actual police can arrive. Again, this stacks the deck in law enforcements hands; allowing them too better prepare, and to track suspects as they flee the scene.

Unfortunately, systems like this allow for extreme abuses in power by those who are entrusted with these advantages. and there needs to be personal, professional, and criminal accountability

Conclusion

Not every case will see the inside of a court room, at least not as a judge or jury trial. More will see a preliminary hearing, which for all intents and purposes is a mini trial; the scope of these events differs from court to court. Moreover, a few others may be presented to a Grand Jury. But only a small percentage will actually go to trial.

Unfortunately, not all cases can go to trial. There simply aren't enough resources, and the court's time is absolutely precious. New officers should also remember, that once the case has been referred to the prosecutor's office, their job, for the most part is done. Officers not to let it go, and allow their counterparts do their job, and adjudicate it as best they can: Dismiss, plea, or try.

The goal of any officer should be to provide the prosecutors with the best possible case; understanding that there are no perfect cases. Again, all cases have their strengths and weakness; hopefully the officer has done their best to address each point.

The prosecutor's job is to weigh these points against other factors, and decide which cases to try. If a case is pled out earlier in the process, hopefully it's because a prosecutor chose too, not because they had too. In that way, the police officer writing these reports can have a significant impact on those decisions; and in that they have a significant impact on the lives of the people that they are paid to serve and protect.

Good luck, you'll need it.

Appendix A

YOU SIGNED IT; YOU OWN IT!

Written by Jan Mirikitani
jbcnsltg@hotmail.com

PROFESSIONAL REPORT WRITING SKILL CHECKLIST

Public Contact skills:

1. Human civility & courtesy

2. Officer presence, appearance, & bearing

3. Strive to build positive rapport

Communication Skills for information gathering:

1. Initial statements set a baseline; be respectful regardless of what you believe.

2. Interviews: use closed, open, layered, hypothetical, & guilt-seeking questions

3. Active listening: paraphrase back to establish accuracy

4. List initial observations of victim & scene

5. Ask victim for statement for stolen phone, credit cards, bank cards, etc.

Writing Skills for report writing:

1. Note-taking: organized, legible, use short-hand, use larger surface when possible. Use face sheets for complete pedigree and specific thefts.

2. Grammatical: number, agreement, case, sentences, punctuation, spelling

3. Rename the noun to avoid unclear pronouns.

4. Use active voice of the verb to retain chain of custody of quotes and evidence.

5. Write clear sentences; one idea per sentence (less than 15 words).

6. Use accurate, clear, concise words, not police jargon.

7. Build MO: specifically describe crime scene, method of entry, stolen property, etc.

8. Proof and edit for accuracy, completeness, grammar, spelling, & clarity.

Report should justify Officer actions on scene & be legally correct.

1. Elements of the crime: 5 W's & 1 H

2. Quote the law, ordinance, SOP, training terms.

3. Be clear on who gave Miranda Warning when, by whom, signature/date, etc.

4. Attach victim, witness, suspect statements signed & dated.

Organization:

1. Chronological order: follow the reporting Officer from start to finish.

2. Paragraphs: topic sentence clarifies content, internal organization/time order.

3. Transitions: state when the Officer changes action, location, introduce new people.

4. Methods for handling scene, preserving evidence, searching house, canvass.

DON'T LIE!! It is a lie to copy & paste a report & change names & addresses.

DON'T LIE about AREA CANVASS. List the addresses & persons contacted.

ELEMENTS OF THE CRIME

WHO?

Discovered the crime? Reported the crime?

Identify victim(s)? Witness(es)? Leads?

Had a motive: probable suspect(s)?

Who found victim? Who saw victim alive last?

WHAT?

Happened (victim's original statement + Officer's interview)?

Crime: the elements of this crime (see Blue Legal Handbook)?

Implicates suspect: Motive? Equipment used? Weapons? Vehicle and transportation?

Look for M.O. Type of assault on victim? Type of entry/damage to property?

Witnesses: original statements + Officer interviews. What they saw, heard, know?

Physical evidence: Officer observations? Collection methods?

WHERE?

Crime scene location(s)?

Was crime discovered?

Was the victim? Witness(es)?

Was suspect interviewed, arrested?

Did Officer conduct canvass (names/addresses/statements)?

WHEN?

Was the crime committed? Was the crime discovered?

Timeline from victim, witness, suspect statements & officer interviews.

Was suspect arrested?

HOW?

Was there a crime committed?

Did the victim appear? Did the property look (M.O.)?

Did suspect leave the crime scene? Point of entry, point of exit?

Did suspect use equipment & weapons (M.O.)?

WHY?

Was crime committed? Officer's conclusions from facts observed + victim, witness, suspect interviews, canvass? Victim's cooperation or reluctance to assist reporting Officer?

Officers must OWN their reports/investigation/work quality:

Field Trainers & Sergeants should edit reports prudently. Corrections can save the Officer & Department from embarrassment down the line. Always explain the reasons for required changes to the writing Officer.

What Officers Should Clearly Articulate

1. Write *legible complete* notes on scene: key to accurate, complete reports. *If you can't read your writing, your notes are worthless!*

2. Explain reason for contact. Include dispatcher's information.

3. Initial observations of scene & complainant's physical appearance & emotional state.

4. Note complainant's initial statement is crucial if the investigation turns.

5. Get statements from victim(s), witness(es), & suspect(s); as a baseline for truth.

6. Officer walk-through/protective sweep: state your instructions to resident>

   a. First clear the scene to determine if suspect is still on premise.

   b. Victim walk-through to determine nature/extent of crime/what's missing/disturbed?

   c. Safe-guard potential physical evidence.

7. Get complete & accurate pedigree of victim(s), witness(es), & suspect(s).

   a. State whole name in narrative; then follow SOP for how names should be stated.

   b. Witness statements: ask where witness was when he/she saw/heard this. Verify if that's possible (while still on scene). Document both in report.

8. Elements of the crime must be clearly stated. Name the crime; verify in Blue Book.

   a. Reasonable suspicion & probable cause must be clearly stated.

   b. Officers should know & be able to explain how/why suspected was arrested.

   c. Give clear concise description of a suspect's actions. Don't use police jargon.

9. Secure crime scene; all crime scenes are contaminated. Bigger is better!

   a. Establish physical boundaries: yellow tape, lock/block door, etc.

   b. List name/rank of who crosses tape/reason for access. Restrict unauthorized people.

   c. Use methodical search for physical evidence. Lift prints, photograph, collect hair, blood, fibers, nail scrapings, fluids w/proper procedures. Take elimination prints.

   d. Preserve & document evidence: bagged or boxed, tagged, logged, & secured in accordance to SOPs for chain of custody. Sign, date, & complete evident receipts.

   e. Avoid time-lapse when transporting evidence to station.

10. Canvass for leads. Be clear about who said what about whom to whom. Secure as much re-contact information (names/addresses, who was not home during canvass, but home at time of incident). Don't provide information about the criminal incident.

ACCURATE: No cut & paste. Never lie. Falsifying report content is perjury.

CLEAR: If you can't understand the narrative, clear up the wording.

CHRONOLOGICAL: Officer's report must reflect the order of handling/investigation.

COMPLETE: are all elements & key information there? If information is missing, have Officer go get it. Officers should see the report's role in arrest & prosecution.

TIME: Use your time judiciously; delays can equal loss.

1. Get information together in a timely manner, b/c review/editing will happen soon: Supervisors, Detectives, Commanders, Chief/Sheriff, Prosecutors, public.

2. Juvenile(s) in custody: adhere to the all legal perimeters.

REPORT REQUISITES FOR SUCCESSFUL INVESTIGATION > PROSECUTION

1. Attention to detail: work the case & write report like victim is your family.

2. Pursue obvious leads, especially when time sensitive.

3. Always obtain current & accurate information: name, DOB, cell #, e-mail address, home address, a parent (if you can get it). *Do not rely on what is in the computer.*

4. Always get the who, what, where, when, why, & how.

PROPERTY CRIMES:

Do while on scene if at all possible:

1. Get value of damage/of stolen item. If unknown, have victim get you a value estimate.

2. Photograph recovered property with detail, especially when returning it to owner.

3. Do a canvass; properly document addresses, names, & re-contact information.

ASSAULT:

1. Observable injuries and/or complaints of injuries

2. Officer's observations of scene (turned over furniture, broken items, weapons, etc.)

3. Victim & Suspect demeanor & statements

4. Indications of alcohol and/or drugs

5. Detailed witness statements

6. Relationships of Victim/Suspect/Witness

7. Medical care & records documentation

8. Justifications: trespasser, defense of others, defense of property, etc.

ASSAULT WITH A DEADLY WEAPON:

1. <u>Complete description of weapon:</u>

   a. <u>Knife</u>: type, hilt, blade length & type, biological evidence observed, location found

b. <u>Firearm</u>: type, make, model, serial number, action, ammunition, condition found: hammer cocked, biological evidence, operational condition

c. Anything that could be used as a deadly weapon: brick, chemicals, hammer, pipe, etc.

2. <u>Special conditions for firearm possession:</u>

a. Mental illness documentation

b. Felony convictions

c. Protection Orders

d. Domestic Violence convictions

e. Dishonorable Military Discharge

3. <u>Castle Doctrine considerations: home & vehicle</u>

a. Weapon operational

b. Shell casing location(s)

c. Wound description: muzzle impression, stippling, etc.

d. Dexterity of shooter: left vs right

e. Holster present; gun case present & location

BURGLARY/ATTEMPTS

1. Description of scene location (critical/perishable).

2. Suspect's method of entry & exit (forced, outer door, broken window, etc.)

3. Suspected activity inside building (drawers rummaged, food eaten, etc.)

4. Suspicious activity outside building (screens cut, marks on outer door, tampered exterior lighting, footprints/shoe size/type, etc.).

5. Prior suspicious or unusual activity on street, around building, vehicles.

6. Thorough & documented area canvass (names, addresses, phone #s, feedback)

7. Fully document & describe the property taken & where it was taken from.

8. Time frame of the occurrence.

9. Document processing & description of crime scene, photos, physical evidence collected

10. If you can't thoroughly &/or accurately depict locations, use available resources (Google Maps, residential floor plan) to map observations.

CAR CLOUTING/CAR BURGLARY:

1. Single or multiple vehicles involved

2. Scene location: business parking lot, apartment complex, residential street, etc.

3. Time of day, weather conditions

4. Method of entry into cars, locked or unlocked

5. Complete description of items stolen & interior compartment areas targeted

6. Biological evidence at scene: fingerprint impressions, glove impressions, blood

7. Debris on exterior of vehicle or on ground near vehicle

8. Computer information including WIFI accounts used or profile information

9. Was crime scene processed?

CIT/Mental Health Subject

1. Fully describe appearance, behaviors, words, & actions of CIT subject.

2. Write detailed interview with family member(s)/care-giver/friend, etc.

3. Detail previous Police contact with subject (dates, locations, what occurred).

4. List all prescribed medications & self-medication.

5. List all known doctors, counselors, treatment, & contact information for each.

6. Describe subject's living environment & subject's destruction (if any).

7. Complete a CIT form as thoroughly as possible.

IDENTITY THEFT:

1. Document venue/jurisdiction.

2. Manner of theft, open account in victim's name, purchases

3. ID used by suspect: social security #, full name, partial name, date of birth

4. How victim was notified of theft

5. Document credit bureau reports

6. Fully document account numbers, purchase locations, delivery addresses, etc.

INVASION OF PRIVACY (Peeping Tom):

1. Document time of day of occurrence.

2. Document suspicious occurrences: gates left open, items under windows (cigarettes, gum wrappers, shoe prints), motion lights activated, strange noises, barking dogs.

3. Known stalkers

4. Document other calls for suspicious vehicles, people in the area.

SHOPLIFTING:

1. Summary of Loss Prevention Officer's report

2. Document Miranda Warning if in custody.

3. Describe method used by suspect for concealing or removing items.

4. Describe suspicious actions & indications of accomplices

5. Full description of stolen items & their value

6. Summary of video surveillance

7. Previous encounters between business & suspect(s)

8. Document of no trespass orders

9. Document any related crimes in narrative.

VANDALISM (possibility of hate crime):

1. Document in detail type of damage: broken, spray painted, scratched, etc.

2. Document damage to victim: message: racial, ethnic, religious, sexual words/symbols

3. Document date(s) of vandalism: prior history

4. On-going disputes with anyone

5. Communications that could indicate motive; collect tapes, emails, letters, etc.

6. Document if crime scene was processed.

7. Verify canvass to see if there are other victims or solely this victim.

CRIMES AGAINST PERSONS cases:

1. Victim's/witness' description of suspect; personal show-up ID is best, if available.

2. Officer's initial observations of scene & victim

3. Photographs/video of scene; preservation of scene & evidence: cell phones, gun-shot residue, finger-prints, DNA, body fluids.

4. Neighborhood canvass: address, apt #s, names, phone #s, what was seen/heard.

5. Document spontaneous utterances (if possible, on tape) of victim/suspect verbatim

CHILD (PHYSICAL) ABUSE:

1. Document clear & accurate conditions of scene. Take photographs.

2. Identify & photograph all injuries. Preserve potential evidence. Was medical treatment received? Get details.

3. If child is verbal, CAC interview is preferred option.

4. Document witness statements well (could be potential suspect later).

5. Notify DCFS, if applicable.

DEATH INVESTIGATION:

1. Begin every death investigation as a Homicide, until it is proven otherwise. Something that appears insignificant may be very important later in the case.

2. Scene documentation: evidence, photographs, potential witnesses, suspects.

SUDDEN vs SUSPICIOUS DEATH:

1. Who found the body, relationship to deceased, how they obtained entry

2. Description of room: Normal? Struggle? Medications? Ransacked?

3. Description of body: Injuries? Blood? Bruising? Where body was laying.

4. All child/adolescent deaths are suspicious.

DRUG INVESTIGATIONS:

1. List where the drugs were specifically found, weight (ask your State's Attorney), field test results.

2. Send to lab for felony cases & for unknown substance.

3. List any spontaneous statements made by offender indicating possession.

POSSESSION WITH INTENT TO DELIVER:

1. Document lack of drug paraphernalia to use the drugs.

2. If currency is seized/possessed, document how money was kept (folded specific way/ separated from other money, many small bills) = details may indicate drug sales.

3. How drugs are packaged & weights per package.

4. List spontaneous statements/booking questions/responses.

5. Charge suspect with possession w/intent within 1000 feet of protected property, if it pertains (church, housing project, school). Distance can be calculated on 911 screen.

DOMESTIC VIOLENCE:

1. Victim's appearance, emotions, & statements. Get it NOW; could be influenced later.

2. Document & photograph injuries, including full face shot of victim for identification.

3. Medical treatment if refused/provided (diagnosis, treatment, treating physician, facility.

4. Children often present during these incidents. Depending on case seriousness & child's age, consider calling Division of Children & Family Services or Child Advocacy Center.

Domestic Violence: for Probable Cause Statement

1. Detailed description of physical and/or verbal aggression observed upon arrival.

2. Document previous 911 calls/domestic incidents (reported/unreported) & progression.

3. Document appearance of scene (damaged furniture, holes in walls, etc.)

4. Record through audio/video or written victim statement.

    a. Did suspect threaten the victim? Victim's children? Victim's family?

    b. Was victim prevented from leaving? Physically restrained/how? Took car keys? Disallowed to use a phone? Took victim's money? ID?

    c. Did victim say suspect stalked her/him?

5. Document alcohol &/or drug use of suspect & victim? Was victim coerced? How?

Describe suspect's demeanor when intoxicated &/or high.

6. Does victim remember weapons used? Describe (each) in detail.

7. Clearly describe each person's demeanor & mannerisms during police statements.

Verify if parties are employed/financial dependency.

8. Document who gave victim assistance packets & shelter information.

9. Conduct & document area canvass, especially for non-family witnesses.

Fully explain why an arrest was made/not made. Get recorded/written suspect statements.

SEX CRIME-ADULT VICTIM:

1. Document victim's appearance & emotions.

2. List any potential witnesses/neighborhood canvass/with all re-contact information.

3. Describe the scene. Search for any possible evidence left behind.

4. Describe/document & photograph injuries.

5. Within 48 hours, conduct a BRIEF interview to get summary & assess safety issues.

6. After 48 hours, conduct a detailed audio/video recorded statement.

7. Does victim know the offender? Who? (show-up or photo line-up)

8. Medical treatment/sexual assault kit

9. Officers should not document their own personal opinion of victim.

SEX CRIME-CHILD VICTIM: Use Child Advocacy Center (CAC)

1. Same as adult victim, except for the documented interview.

2. DO NOT interview child victim. Officer may get brief statement if victim knows assailant.

3. Refer victim to CAC for interview.

4. Look for other potential child victims/witnesses who should be interviewed at CAC.

5. Refer to a children's hospital if Sexual Assault/Abuse occurred within 72 hours of report.

6. Detailed statements from reporter of crime or witnesses are necessary.

7. Notify DCFS, if applicable.

FIRST RESPONDING OFFICER MUST PRIORITIZE PERISHABLE EVIDENCE

Perishable Evidence: evidence that won't last, tough to preserve due to temperature, weather, location; best to photograph & state in Officer's report.

Truism: criminals are creatures of habit, use same mode of entry, same methods for getting rid of stolen property. *Catching the criminal = less victims.*

First Responding Officer must:

1. Clearly describe victim's initial observations & scene. Different by time Detectives arrive.

2. Safeguard perishable evidence on victim(s) & scene.

3. Look for M.O. & leads. Photograph & describe concisely.

4. Interview to determine if resident had prior contact with suspect (inside job)

1. Point of entry/exit: describe methods

a. Visibility from street

b. Was door locked/unlocked, strike-plate pry marks, type of lock(s)?

c. Alarms: Was it triggered? Was resident contacted? Signs posted on property?

d. Broken glass: location, direction, prints, blood, fluids/fibers?

e. Door mule-kicked: direction of shoe print, facing or back kicked, size/shape/tread of shoe print, shoulder or hip pushed? Describe what you see.

f. Repairmen access: name of company/employees/contact information. 9

2. Walking property perimeter: note what does/doesn't belong to resident(s)

a. Photograph foot-prints: snow, dew, cut grass, mud, side-walks

b. Find cigarette butts (brand), ashes on sill, behind bushes, gum & wrappers.

c. Check yard & trash cans for bottles/cans/wrappers (DNA & prints)

d. Check driveway for oil spots or debris not caused by resident's vehicle.

3. Verify firearms on site:

a. Type, name, model, & caliber; licensed? Storage? Locked? Who knew location?

4. Rooms ransacked: What's Missing? Which rooms?

a. Describe M.O., familiarity with property location, if possessions are stacked, strewn.

b. Did thief use victim's pillowcase, gym bag, purse to haul stolen property?

5. Prints on where stolen property was located:

a. Check toilet seat & faucet handles for prints (female dwellers).

b. Are gloves missing from residence: jersey, leather, what color?

6. Photograph inside, street side, back, street access. Protect blood & bodily fluids, droplets & spatter.

Appendix B

GRAMMAR REVIEW
PARTS OF SPEECH, PUNCTUATION, PARAGRAPHS, STRONG CLEAR SENTENCES

Written by Jan Mirikitani

Parts of speech:

Nouns, pronouns, verbs, adjectives, adverbs, prepositions, conjunctions, interjections.

Primary marks of punctuation:

Apostrophe, colon, comma, exclamation point, parentheses, periods, question mark, quotation marks, semi-colon

Key Concepts:

Number = singular & plural

Agreement = number must be consistent in that sentence.

Case = nominative, possessive, objective

Tense = time (present, past, past participle, future tense)

Voice = active & passive voice of the verb.

NOUNS

1. Proper nouns are capitalized: name of *a particular* person, place, thing, or event.

Days of the week & months of the year are capitalized. Seasons are not capitalized. Ex: Sam Meyer, Christmas, Walgreens, Winter-Fest, Ballwin Summer Days

Directions are not capitalized unless direction is part of the street name. Ex: He drove **s**outh on Maple. The knife was found in the **n**ortheast corner of the shed.

I followed the subject's vehicle on **N**orth Lindbergh Boulevard.

All legal charges are capitalized: Larceny, Aggravated Battery. Could be all caps too.

Branding: businesses, restaurants, retail, companies; could be all caps, all lower case, spelled uniquely/wrong. Put in brackets **[ ]** the first time if spelled incorrectly.

Acronyms: Write out what it stands for; place abbreviation in parenthesis.

Federal Bureau of Investigation (FBI, P.O.S.T., OC, D.A.R.E.)

2. Common nouns: name of no particular person, place, thing, or event. Ex: autumn, bike, child, drugs, man, festival, food, north, south, eastbound

3. Compound nouns: 2+ words form a unit; some are hyphenated, some proper nouns. Ex: w/hyphen: all in-laws, all 2-word numbers between 21-99 Ex: w/no hyphen: high school, table lamp, arm chair, situational ethics, nonverbals Proper nouns: Labor Day, Peace Corps, Veterans Administration

4. Collective nouns: group name (singular or plural) that must be in agreement with the verb, pronouns, & modifiers in that sentence. Ex: team, jury, squad, family Ex: The jury delivered ***its*** *verdict.* The judge thanks the juror**s** for ***their*** service.

PRONOUNS

A pronoun *takes the place* of a noun.

The noun the pronoun replaces is called the antecedent.

If the noun antecedent is singular, the pronoun *must be* singular (agree in number). Ex: Joe said *he* would wait with Billy for *his* bus. (singular) Ex: Mary, Sue, & Cindy were in the hall when *they* heard the bell ring. (plural)

If the noun antecedent is plural, the pronoun must be plural (agree in number).

The Manager ordered all squads to report with **their duty belts**.

Singular Personal Pronouns:

Nominative Case (subject)	Possessive Case	Objective Case (object)
I	my, mine	me
you	your(s)	you
he, she, it	his, her(s) its	him, her, it

Plural Personal Pronouns:

Nominative Case	Possessive Case	Objective Case
we	our(s)	us
you	your(s)	you
they	their(s)	them

Relative Pronouns:

People: who, whom, whose, which. Ex: Ex: The man *to whom* I spoke is here. *Who* lost their ticket? *Whose* wallet is this?

Places, objects, & events: this, that (singular), **these, those** (plural). Ex: *These* books are Marcy's; *that* folder is Sam's.

WHOM is *always* preceded by a preposition: by whom, for whom, from whom, to whom

Indefinite pronouns-singular or plural: verb & modifier must be *in agreement.*

Singular: each, any, anybody, anyone, anything, every, everybody, everyone, everything, nobody, no one, not one, none. Ex: *Each* squad, *any* officer, *every* student, *not one* player, *no one* is here

Plural: all, several, some, many, most. Ex: all squads, several officers, some students, many civilians, most Commanders

VERBS: VOICE, NUMBER, TENSE

A sentence contains a subject & verb.

Active voice : run, sit, stand, hit, kick, punch, throw, think, decide, love, hate

Passive voice: am, is, are, was, were, be, being, been, has, have, had, will, shall

VOICE = active or passive:

Active voice uses simple sentence order: **subject + verb + object**. Ex: Officer Jones found the pipe in the glove box. (States *who did what?)*

Passive voice *begins with the object & often fails to name the subject*.

Bad for Police narratives. Ex: The knife was found in the glove box. (Begs the question: Who found the knife

NUMBER = singular or plural passive voice verbs

Singular being verbs: am, is, was, be, being, been, has, had, shall. Ex: I am, she is, Mark was, let her be, she is being crabby, I had, Carrie shall

Plural being verbs: are, were, be, being, been, have, had, will. Ex: *Aaron & Mike* are, *The boys* were, *Residents* have

Rules for singular/plural:

1. If subject is singular, use singular verb; if subject is plural, use plural verb. Ex: The test questions *were* difficult. The box of books *is* missing.

2. Singular verbs end in s or es. Add "s" to the verb for a singular subject. Ex: Levi walks to school every day. He plays soccer.

3. When 2 subjects are joined with a conjunction, verb must agree with last noun named. Ex: Neither the victim or witnesses *need* medical attention. (not *needs*)

TENSE = time of the action

Regular verbs form the past tense by adding 'ed' or 'ied.' Ex: walk/walked, wave/waved, study/studied

Irregular verbs change form in different tenses:

Present, past, participle, past perfect, future. Ex: sing (present), sang (past), singing (present participle), sung (past participle), has/had sung (past perfect), shall/will sing (future)

KEEP TENSE CONSISTENT in a sentence:

The volunteers *came* early and *stayed* late.

The Officer *asked* Walker for his license & *told* him to remain in his vehicle.

Rules for Using VERBS in Police Reports

1. Police reports are mostly written in past tense. Quotes could be present or future tense.

2. Past tense of **REGULAR VERBS** is formed by adding "ed": called, coughed, stopped.

3. **IRREGULAR VERBS** are **CONJUGATED** & change form moving from present to past to past perfect tense. The past participle needs a helper verb (Ex: has, have, had). Verbs ending in "y", past tense adds "ied" *pry/pried.*

4. **Use the ACTIVE VOICE of the verb *to retain the chain of custody.*** Ex: "**I** handcuffed the suspect and transported him to the station."

PASSIVE VOICE breaks the chain of custody. "Suspect was cuffed." By whom?

CONJUGATED IRREGULAR VERBS

Present Tense	Past Tense	Past Participle
am, is, are	was, were	been
beat	beat	beaten
begin	began	begun
bite	bit	bitten
blow	blew	blown
break	broke	broken
bring	brought	brought
buy	bought	bought
can	could	could
choose	chose	chosen
come	came	come
creep	crept	crept
deal	dealt	dealt
do	did	done
draw	drew	drawn
drink	drank	drunk
drive	drove	driven
dry	dried	dried
eat	ate	eaten
fall	fell	fallen

find	found	found
fly	flew	flown
freeze	froze	frozen
get	got	gotten
give	gave	given
go	went	gone
grow	grew	grown
has	had	had
hold	held	held
keep	kept	kept
know	knew	known
lay/lie	laid/lay	laid/lain
leave	left	left
lend	lent	lent
light	lit	lit
lose	lost	lost
make	made	made
read	read	read
ride	rode	ridden
ring	rang	rung
rise	rose	risen
run	ran	run
say	said	said
see	saw	seen
send	sent	sent
shake	shook	shaken
show	showed	shown
sit	sat	sat
sleep	slept	slept
speak	spoke	spoken
spring	sprang	sprung
stand	stood	stood
steal	stole	stolen
swear	swore	sworn
swell	swelled	swollen
swim	swam	swum

swing	swung	swung
take	took	taken
teach	taught	taught
tear	tore	torn
throw	threw	thrown
wear	wore	worn
weep	wept	wept
win	won	won
write	wrote	written

ADJECTIVES & ADVERBS:

Adjectives describe nouns & pronouns & should be concise for clear meaning. Ex: The red 4-door Toyota Tundra pick-up truck was stolen.

Article Adjectives = a, an, the

1. Use *a* if word begins with a consonant: a ball, a car, a doctor, a knife, a gun

2. Use *an* if word begins with a vowel: an alley, an easy, an idea, an old man, an ulcer

3. *The* can be used with words that begin with vowels or consonants. Al said he dropped the ***key*** near the ***garage***.

Adverbs describe verbs, adjectives, & other adverbs. Ex: She is so *tired.* She is always *fair.* She ran fast. He hurried home very *quickly*.

MISPLACED MODIFIERS alter sentence meaning:

Modifiers should be as close to the word they describe as possible for clear meaning.

Correct: Joan bought a blender at Walmart last week, but returned it today.

Wrong: Joan returned the blender to Walmart, that she bought last week.

CONJUNCTIONS: act as COMBINING words for words, phrases, & clauses.

Coordinating conjunctions join words, phrases, & clauses: **and, but, or, so, because**. Ex: He brought his flashlight and vest to roll-call. Choose an apple or a banana.

Correlative conjunctions are used in pairs to make a choice: Ex: either/or, neither/nor, both/and, whether/or not, not only/but also.

Conjunctive adverbs act as conjunctions when they join 2 independent clauses: Ex: as a result, consequently, however, subsequently, therefore, thus. Ex: I told him he had a right to an attorney; *however*, he made a statement.

INTERJECTIONS: express strong feelings or surprise; followed by an exclamation mark. Ex: oh, hey, yikes, wow. Profanity, racist/ethnic/sexist/religious slurs are interjections.

PREPOSITIONS: show DIRECTION or LOCATIONS. Ex: *at* the party, *behind* the wall, *by* the door, *for* his parents, *in* the closet, *inside* the box, *on* the ledge, *over* the fence

Use *between* to separate two people, places, or things.Ex: The child sat *between* his parents. He stood *between* his father and mother.

Use *among* to separate 3 or more things Ex: *Among* his many possessions, his camera was his favorite.

Use *in* when you mean ***inside or within*** a specific location.Ex: I found a knife *in* the box. Use *into* when you move *from the outside to the inside*. Ex: I followed him *into* the kitchen.

Use *to* or *toward* *when you are moving in that direction*. Ex: I drove *to* the victim's vehicle. I walked cautiously *toward* the basement door

Use *at* *when you are there*. Ex: I was *at* the station when the call was received.

Avoid double prepositions: *off of, off from, up against* Use both if true.

He fell *off* the ledge. She jumped *from* the ledge. He pushed him *up against* the wall.

Only **use objective case pronouns** after a preposition. Ex: He did it *for me* (not *I*). The gift is for her (not *she*)

PREPOSITIONS:

About, above, after, against, among, around, at, before, behind, beneath, beside, between, by = (next to, in close proximity to) down, during, for, from, in, into, of, on, out, outside, over, through, to, toward(s), under, up, upon, upwards, with, without

about: I asked *about* Fred's health.

above: I found the key *above* the door frame.

after: Sam left *after* work.

against: Jack leaned *against* the wall.

among: involves more than 2: He stood among his friends.

around: Jake looked around the room for his wallet.

at: Supervisor Peters was at the scene when I arrived.

before: I stood *before* the Manager.

behind: Tommy hid *behind* the sofa.

beneath, under, underneath all mean the same thing:

We found a toddler hiding *beneath* the basement steps/*underneath* the steps.

We looked *under* the basement steps for the toddler.

by, beside, & next to <u>are very similar</u>.

Mary sat *beside* Dan in the lobby. Mary sat *next to* Dan in the lobby.

I saw the suspect standing *by* his vehicle.

down: I looked *down* the hallway *towards* the kitchen.

during: She cried *during* the interview.

for: I did it *for* you. This bone is *for* the dog.

from: The letter is *from* George. I received the box *from* Sue.

in: The ruler is *in* my top desk-drawer.

into: I walked *into* his office.

of: The box *of* flowers are *for* you.

on: I left the car keys *on* the dresser.

out: I looked *out* the window.

outside: Joe looked *outside towards* the back gate.

over: The horse jumped *over* the fence.

through: The bride & groom walked *through* the arch together.

to: Please, give the book *to* me. When you go *to* the store, please buy milk.

toward(s): A cat ran *towards* the headlights. (singular subject add an "s") Joe & Pete walked *toward* the house. (plural subject/no "s")

under: Troy looked *under* the bed for the suitcase.

up: Stand *up* when the flag is passing.

upon: The doctor asked the patient *to* sit upon the table.

with: Sit *with* them. Come *with* me. I will go *with* him to the store.

without: She was driving *without* a license.

PARAGRAPHS ORGANIZE & SEPARATE IDEAS

1. Paragraphs.

Start a NEW paragraph when the Officer changes location, action, or talks to a new person, or if it's a new topic.

2. **TOPIC SENTENCE**: starts every paragraph with a roadmap for paragraph content.

3. **PARAGRAPH COHERENCE**: logical/chronological ordering of sentence information in that paragraph.

4. **TRANSITIONAL STATEMENTS**: Paragraphs should end or begin with a sentence that bridges one paragraph to the next. Tells reader Officer's location & actions.

   a. Location: across the street, behind the car, nearby, under the steps

   b. Number/time order: first/initially/upon arrival, second, after that, next, when, then, finally/lastly, earlier, later, the next day, that morning/ afternoon/night

5. Sergeant/Detective should be able to skim paragraphs & quickly find topic content.

WRITE STRONG SENTENCES FOR CLEAR CONCISE MEANING.

4 TYPES OF SENTENCES FOR MEANING:

1. Declarative: makes a statement; ends with a period (.).

2. Interrogative: asks a question; ends with a question mark (?).

3. Imperative: a command; ends with a period (.) or exclamation point (!).

4. Exclamatory: expresses excited feelings; ends with an exclamation point (!).

4 TYPES OF SENTENCE STRUCTURES:

1. Simple sentence: one complete thought; can have more than one subject/verb.

2. Compound sentence: two or more complete thoughts.

3. Complex sentence: one independent & one dependent clause.

4. Compound-complex sentence: two or more dependent/independent clauscs.

KEY CONCEPTS for writing sentences:

1. **FRAGMENT:** group of words punctuated like a sentence, BUT lacks a subject, verb, AND a complete thought.

2. **CLAUSE:** group of words with subject(s) & predicate: verb(s).

Independent clause: subject, verb, & complete meaning.. Ex: I entered the report into the system.

Dependent clause: subject & verb, but NEEDS an independent clause to make sense. Ex: *After* I ate lunch, *I entered the report.*

Dependent clauses begin with subordinating conjunctions. Ex: after, although, because, before, if, since, unless, until, when, while.

CORRECT WORD ORDER for ACCURATE, CLEAR, CONCISE meaning:

Actor + Action + Object Weak structure breaks the chain of custody.

Right: *Sam Hill* found a wallet on the floor in the bathroom. Hill turned it into Public Safety.

Wrong: Security has a wallet found in a bathroom on the fourth floor.

Right: I found the knife under the mattress. I bagged it and transported it to the the Convent.

Wrong: A knife was found under the mattress, was bagged & transported to the the Convent. (Who found the knife, bagged & transported it?)

Avoid JARGON (occupational verbiage) unless you give detailed explanation. Ex: ransacked, tossed, non-compliant, furtive movement, non-responsive

Avoid PRETENTIOUS WORDS; use simple familiar words for clear meaning.

SIMPLE SENTENCE (one complete thought; can have a plural subjects & plural verbs). Ex: Officers Dent & Jones collected the evidence & took it to the station.

3 CORRECT ways to punctuate COMPOUND SENTENCES (2+ independent clauses):

Each example is punctuated correctly.

1. Separate both independent clauses with **a period & capital letter.**

I entered corridor B. I could hear a man's voice from inside the main office.

2. Separate both independent clauses with **BOTH a comma & a conjunction**.

I ran up the steps quickly, because I heard a female yelling for help.

3. Separate both independent clauses with **a semi-colon** (;).

The letter behind the semi-colon remains lower case unless it is a proper noun.

Some Officers type their reports in the station; others use in-car computers

COMPLEX SENTENCES

One dependent + one independent clause separated by a comma:

Subordinating conjunctions: begin dependent clauses in complex sentences.

Ex: after, although, as, because, before, if, since, unless, until, when, while

After I picked up lunch, I drove north on Veterans Parkway.

When you cross the intersection, look for Joe's Bakery.

Before I ended my shift, I completed both of my reports.

If you see Officer Martin, tell him I need his report.

As I entered the garage, I smelled gasoline.

While you are in the station, please give this to the Director.

When you put the independent clause first, no comma is needed.

PUNCTUATION MARKS

Proper use of punctuation impacts meaning & is a sign of literacy professionalism.

APOSTROPHE

1. Used to form possession. Ex: Joe's coat, the family's cabin, the bands' instruments (more than one band)

2. The apostrophe comes *after* names ending in an S (singular or plural) ***with NO added S***. Ex: Adams', Atkins', Cross', Gross', Moss', Phillips', Thomas', Williams', Willis'. Ex: Mary Williams' dog is still missing.

3. When 2+ nouns show possession, *add apostrophe S to the last noun named.*

Ex: Bill, Bob, & Tom's apartment is on Maple Street.

4. Use an apostrophe to represent missing letters in contractions. Ex: can't = cannot, won't = will not, aren't = are not, it's = it is/it was *Officers CANNOT use contractions in police reports; only when quoting someone.*

5. Optional to use in dates: Ex: 1950's or the 1950s; either is acceptable.

COMMA

1. Use a comma *before the conjunction* in a COMPOUND SENTENCE. Ex: We scheduled the program at 7:00 pm***, so*** most parents could attend.

2. Use a comma to SEPARATE a DEPENDENT FROM INDEPENDENT CLAUSE. Ex: If you leave, be sure to lock the door.

3. Use a comma to separate items/phrases/clauses in a SERIES: Ex: Officer Brown traveled to St. Louis, Springfield, & Joplin for training. Ex: Jack drove to the airport, flew to New York, & took a taxi to the hotel. Ex: The Officer interviewed the victim, canvassed for witnesses, & filed her report.

4. Use commas to set off extraneous and helpful information: Ex: The stolen truck, parked behind the cafeteria, was destroyed by fire.

Use commas to set off an appositive (clarifying words that follow noun/pronoun): Ex: Mark Wilson, a Harvard physician, is on our Board of Directors.

5. Use a comma to set off introductory words: accordingly, consequently, thus, furthermore, however, nevertheless, therefore. Ex: We had Probable Cause, nevertheless, we waited for the police.

6. Use a comma after mild interjections, a person's name/title, or yes/no. Ex: *Wow,* can you believe this price! Ex: *Mom,* are you home? Ex: *Yes,* I can give you directions to the station.

7. Use a comma to separate the speaker from a QUOTATION. Ex: Wilson yelled, "If you come in here, you'll be sorry!"

8. Other uses for commas: Ex: After the greeting & closing in a friendly letter or note:

Dear Aunt Grace, Sincerely, Respectfully

To separate date from year: June 5, 2012 No commas in military dates: 5 June 2012 Ex: When writing an address on the same line (not the zip code): 157 Main Street, St. Louis, MO 63145

COLON is always followed by **two typed spaces**.

1. Introduces a quotation (or could use a comma). Ex: Officer Jones radioed: "Send the EMTs to the fourth floor now!"

2. Introduces a list. Ex: Jackson said the following items are missing from his garage:

3. Follows the salutation (greeting) in a business letter. Ex: Dear Sir:

4. Follows each entry of a business memo.

Ex: Date: August 2, 2012

To: Bill Frank, Director, EJI

From: Samuel Height

Re: Invoice for payment

5. Separates main book title from subtitle. Stress: Choosing to Manage It!

6. Separates the publication site from publisher (bibliography). Ex: Camden, NJ: Littleton Press, Inc.

EXCLAMATION POINT

Ending mark of punctuation that follows an excited statement, profanity, racial slurs. Ex: Incredible! I won! Get away from me! Don't ever come back here!

HYPHEN/DASH -

Consult dictionary for accurate usage.

1. To form compound words: Ex: cross-reference, son-in-law, clear-cut, twenty-one, two-thirds, on-going

2. To join some prefixes, suffixes, letters to words: Ex: pre-Civil War era, ex-wife, f-sharp, president-elect, t-shirt, u-turn

3. Use suspended hyphens for hyphenated words in a series: Ex: We interviewed the mother-, father-, and son-in-law.

PARENTHESES ( ):

Used to enclose information that further explains words stated in front of it in sentence. Ex: Jim Cross (owner of Cross Bakery) gave his statement. Ex: Walgreen's (Elm & Watson Road) was burglarized last night.

Commas can be used in the place of parentheses. Ex: Jim Cross, owner of Cross Bakery, gave his statement.

PERIOD

Use a period:

1. To end sentences that are statements, mild commands, & indirect questions. Ex: The Director will speak at the conference in Springfield. Ex: Have a seat in the waiting room. Ex: The instructor asked the Officers if they were ready for their exam.

2. With abbreviations, unless the acronym does not require it. Ex: Mr., Mrs., Ms., Dr., Ph.D., Ln., St., Oct.

Exceptions: postal abbreviations for states: double caps, no periods.

MO, IL, CA, TX, AZ

Exceptions: organizational branding that does not use periods

NBA, AFL-NFL, CBS, IBM, AA

QUESTION MARK:

Ending mark of punctuation that follows a question (interrogative sentence). Ex: Why didn't you call me for a ride?

QUOTATION MARKS

1. Use quotation marks to enclose direct quotes from speaker/writer.

A comma or colon after the speaker & verb are both correct. Ex: The suspect muttered**,** "She had it coming!"

The suspect muttered**:** "She had it coming!"

The following is Smith's statement and is not verbatim. (What does this mean?)

2. Use single quotation marks to enclose a quote within a quote. Ex: Sam Abbott stated: "I heard Morgan yell, 'Stop, Roger!' before the gunshot."

3. If quoting a statement with more than four-typed single-space lines, indent ten spaces, and don't use quotation marks.

4. Use quotation marks in bibliography for the names of published articles, short stories, titles of poems or songs, chapter titles in a book.

But underline or *italicize* the names of publications: books, magazine, newspapers. Ex: In the May issue of The FBI Journal for Law Enforcement, there's an article called "Identity Theft Is Rampant".

A SEMI-COLON cannot be used as a comma.

Separates 2 independent clauses parallel in structure or meaning. Ex: Richards denied ever meeting Sara; his neighbors said he had. Ex: I heard crying as I entered the room; it sounded like a small child.

References

Brooks, M. (ca.1974). Blazing Saddles., 1974

Farrington, D. (2014). St. Louis officers shoot, kill knife-wielding man. MPR News.

https://www.mprnews.org/story/2014/08/19/st-louis-shooting

Ingram, P. (2025). Another grand jury declines to indict ex-Tucson cop for killing man in wheelchair; 3rd attempt by Pima County to prosecute Ryan Remington in 2021 shooting death of Richard Lee Richards is last, Conover says. Tucson Sentinel.

https://www.tucsonsentinel.com/local/report/010925_remington_richards/another-grand-jury-declines-indict-ex-tucson-cop-killing-man-wheelchair/

KGUN News Tucson. (2025). No Grand Jury indictment for former TPD officer in shooting death of man in 2021. news/no-grand-jury-indictment-for-former-tpd-officer-in-shooting-death-of-man-in-2021

KVOA News 4 Tucson. (2023). Former Tucson police officer cleared of manslaughter.

https://www.kvoa.com/townnews/law/former-tucson-police-officer-cleared-of-manslaughter/article_157be086-922c-11ed-9f7c-67494671a54a.html

Levy, G. (2014). Police Shoot Knife-Wielding Suspect in St. Louis. US News.

https://www.upi.com/Top_News/US/2014/08/19/Police-shoot-knife-wielding-suspect-in-St-Louis/9791408473586/

Mirikitani, J. (2024). You Signed it, You Own It. Emailed Document, 109-118.

Mirikitani, Jan. (2024). Grammar Review. Email Document. 119-131

U.S. Constitution. Amendment IV

Hemingway

Faulkner

www.ingramcontent.com/pod-product-compliance
Lightning Source LLC
LaVergne TN
LVHW022058200926
848481LV00003B/972
9798903338672